SEMINAR STUDIES IN HISTORY

DEMOCRACY AND REFORM
1815 – 1885

SEMINAR STUDIES IN HISTORY

DEMOCRACY AND REFORM
1815–1885
D. G. Wright

An imprint of **Pearson Education**

Harlow, England · London · New York · Reading, Massachusetts · San Francisco
Toronto · Don Mills, Ontario · Sydney · Tokyo · Singapore · Hong Kong · Seoul
Taipei · Cape Town · Madrid · Mexico City · Amsterdam · Munich · Paris · Milan

Pearson Education Limited
Edinburgh Gate
Harlow
Essex CM20 2JE
England

and Associated Companies throughout the world

Visit us on the World Wide Web at:
http://www.pearsoneduc.com

First published 1970

ISBN 0-582-31400-3

Transferred to digital print on demand, 2005
Printed and bound by Antony Rowe Ltd, Eastbourne

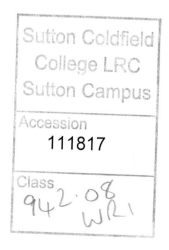

Contents

Introduction to the Series

The seminar method of teaching is being used increasingly in VI forms and at universities. It is a way of learning in smaller groups through discussion, designed both to get away from and to supplement the basic lecture techniques. To be successful, the members of a seminar must be informed, or else—in the unkind phrase of a cynic—it can be a 'pooling of ignorance'. The chapter in the textbook of English or European history by its nature cannot provide material in this depth, but at the same time the full academic work may be too long and perhaps too advanced for students at this level.

For this reason we have invited practising teachers in universities, schools and colleges of further education to contribute short studies on specialised aspects of British and European history with these special needs and pupils of this age in mind. For this series the authors have been asked to provide, in addition to their basic analysis, a full selection of documentary material of all kinds and an up-to-date and comprehensive bibliography. Both these sections are referred to in the text, but it is hoped that they will prove to be valuable teaching and learning aids in themselves.

Note on the System of References:

A bold number in round brackets (5) in the text refers the reader to the corresponding entry in the Bibliography section at the end of the book.

A bold number in square brackets, preceded by 'doc.' [**doc. 6**] refers the reader to the corresponding items in the section of Documents, which follows the main text.

PATRICK RICHARDSON
General Editor

For Victoria

Part One

INTRODUCTION

1 The Background

Modern Britain is a representative parliamentary democracy. Electors vote for the 'image' of a party, or even its leader, rather than for a particular candidate judged on his own merits. A government is formed by the party which obtains a majority of seats at a general election. Until the next election, effective power rests in the hands of the Prime Minister, as leader of the party, and his chief Cabinet ministers. The genuine political power of the monarch and the House of Lords is minimal. Assisted by a large and politically neutral civil service, central government has assumed a pervasive influence over the lives of the people since the mid-nineteenth century.

General elections, held by law every five years (though in practice rather more often) are really general, since the vast majority of seats are contested. They also constitute a genuine 'appeal to the people', for voting is by universal adult suffrage, with only minor exceptions. Again, most adults can stand for election, although prohibited groups are rather more numerous than those disqualified from voting. In practice, chances of election are remote unless a candidate has been adopted by one of the main parties. Modern British politics are dominated by the great party machines, which closely link constituency parties to those in Parliament. Constituencies return only one member, although they still vary considerably in size. Election expenses are subject to a strict legal limit and there are stringent laws against electoral corruption. Voting is by secret ballot (**16**).

While the present electoral system had assumed its basic shape by 1918 (**189**), both the system and the constitution itself were very different in the eighteenth century (**1**). Electors did not vote for political parties and national programmes. General elections, held at least every seven years under the Septennial Act of 1716, were not occasions when the people, or rather the small proportion of them which could vote, chose a ministry. Ministers were appointed by the

3

monarch and elections provided a ministry with the opportunity to confirm itself in power (**34,** ch. 4). Voters chose Members of Parliament and normally based their choice on personal and local, rather than national issues. Elections were certainly not a struggle for mastery between two opposing parties, for there were no great political parties in the modern sense, obedient to their leaders and organised on a national basis for the pursuit of certain policies (**31,** ch. 1; **33,** ch. 20).

It is true that the terms 'Whig' and 'Tory' were used, but normally only of the front bench professional politicians, those who were organised in small groups based on friendship, blood or marriage ties (Melbourne once exclaimed 'Damn the Whigs, they're all cousins!'), or a rather vague sharing of attitudes. Genuine party rivalry, often very bitter, had existed during the reigns of William III and Anne; but the long Whig supremacy after 1715 had robbed party labels of most of their meaning and by 1750 only a discontented rump of politicians continued to call themselves Tory (**35**). However, the 'professional' politicians accounted for only one section of the House. There were also between a hundred and two hundred 'placemen' or 'King's Friends'. Almost invariably they supported the King's government, since they were financially dependent on it. Their numbers included court officers, civil servants, government contractors, army and naval officers, those holding government pensions and sinecures and those sitting for government boroughs. Finally, there were the mass of independent members who formed a majority of the eighteenth-century House of Commons. Some were lawyers and merchants, but most were country gentlemen. Like the King's Friends, though motivated more by a sense of duty than by the desire for material gain, the country gentlemen tended to support the government. They disliked placemen, suspected 'politicians' and regarded parliamentary business as essentially a part-time activity (**33**, ch. 5). Yet no ministry could ever be certain of the allegiance of the country gentlemen and it was certain to fall if their support were withdrawn.

The powers of the monarchy and the House of Lords were much greater than they are nowadays and an integral part of the workings of government. It is, perhaps, worth noting that in the eighteenth century the role of the central government was extremely limited by modern standards. Administrations contented themselves with maintaining law and order, raising taxes, conducting foreign policy and defending the realm. They did not regard it as their function to supervise or direct the economy, or to deal with problems like health, housing, education, poverty and unemployment. If such matters were dealt with at all, they were handled at a local level, mainly by justices of the peace (**1**, ch. 4).

'The King's Government' was no empty phrase in the eighteenth century. Executive power, now in the hands of the Prime Minister, then rested with the monarch, who selected his ministers and exerted major influence on policy (**34**). But Parliament controlled the purse strings and hence the means of carrying out royal policy. Parliamentary support was, therefore, essential for the king's ministers. The king's direct influence over the Commons, through the placemen, was not sufficient to enable him to carry on government against the inflexible opposition of the lower House. Neither could the Commons force on the king ministers he disliked; at least not for long (**1**, ch. 2; **33**, ch. 20). It was the same with policies. George III was forced to end the American War, but was later to cause more than one political crisis by his opposition to Catholic emancipation. Although the power of the monarch began to decline during the last quarter of the century, it remained strong. So did that of the peers. While the House of Commons was stronger than the Lords, because of its representative nature and its exclusive right to initiate financial measures, the upper House had enough power to lend some credence to Blackstone's theory of 'checks and balances' (**34**, ch. 2). Frequently it joined the king in opposing measures passed by the Commons. Most ministers sat in the Lords; so also did the great landed proprietors, whose property included control of many constituencies. Sir Lewis Namier calculated that in 1761 the election of 111 members of the Commons was influenced by 55 peers (**31**, ch. 2). Leaders of the army, navy, civil service, Church and local government also sat in the Lords. Each had the right to proffer advice to the monarch.

Parliamentary constituencies were genuine historical communities, unlike the somewhat artificial units of today. They were divided into two groups: the boroughs and the counties. Most boroughs and each of the counties sent two members to Westminster. By an Act of 1710 a county member had to possess an assured annual income from land of £600; for borough members it was £300. In the eighteenth century there were 558 seats: 489 in England, 24 in Wales and 45 in Scotland. There were 122 members for counties and

432 for boroughs. Voters in county elections had to possess a 'free-hold' worth 40*s*. This sum had been fixed in 1430 and the subsequent decline in the value of money meant that the franchise was a relatively wide one. 'Freehold' could mean land, posts in Church and state, or a guaranteed annual cash income. The fact that each county sent two members ignored population. In 1761 Yorkshire had over 15,000 electors and Rutland only 609.

County elections were dominated by the landed gentry and the aristocracy, although urban and trading interests existed in the home counties, some western counties and in Yorkshire (**38**). The Government also exerted some influence in Hampshire and Kent through the royal dockyards, and in Cornwall through the revenue officers (**31**, ch. 2). 'Influence' is the key word. Crude methods of bribery, employed in some boroughs, were normally regarded as beneath the dignity of the counties. Great landed families usually monopolised the county seats. Often two of the leading families would agree to share the representation and avoid the ruinous costs of a contested election. In 1761 only four counties were contested; only two in 1780. Northamptonshire was contested only four times at thirty-five elections between 1708 and 1832. When agreements broke down, pockets were emptied. The contested Oxfordshire election of 1754 cost £40,000. Sir William Geary spent £22,000 in Kent at the 1776 and 1802 elections. The great Yorkshire election of 1807 cost Earl Fitzwilliam £97,000, the Earl of Harewood £94,000 and William Wilberforce £30,000 (**40**).

Normally, however, there was no need to go to the trouble and expense of a contest. Deference to social superiors was so strong that tenants, shopkeepers, tradesmen and professional men were rarely willing to oppose the wishes of the landed magnates. Thus it was seldom necessary for the latter to resort to sanctions: eviction of tenants, withdrawal of custom from tradesmen and shopkeepers, the withholding of fees owed to solicitors, doctors and land agents. Open voting made rebels easily identifiable. Perhaps not more than one county voter in every twenty was able to exercise his franchise freely.

Boroughs varied a great deal in size and in voting qualifications. Only twenty-two of the 203 English boroughs had over 1000 voters; twenty-two had between 500 and 1000; eleven had 500 or so. The majority of the other 148 were 'rotten' or 'pocket' boroughs; that is, they were influenced or controlled by a patron or by the government. Some boroughs were tiny. All twenty-one in Cornwall, and most of those in Surrey and Sussex, had under 200 electors. Gatton had only six.

There were five main classes of borough. 'Potwalloper' boroughs had votes for all who had their own house and fireplace; they could be small, but included many of the largest boroughs, where elections were most like modern ones. 'Scot and lot' boroughs, like Northampton, were similar; here the vote was held by all male householders who paid local rates and were not on poor relief. In 'freeman boroughs', like East Retford, a freeman qualification could usually be procured by inheritance, marriage, apprenticeship, or even purchase. 'Corporation boroughs' like Bodmin and Bury St Edmunds restricted the franchise to a closed oligarchy of members of the corporation. They were normally self-elected and frequently non-resident. In 'burgage boroughs' the franchise was attached to a piece of land; whoever owned that piece of land could vote. The most notorious of these was Old Sarum, a mound in Wiltshire with no houses. On election day, the seven voters met in a tent specially erected for the purpose.

Like the counties, the boroughs were open to 'influence', usually of a cruder sort. Again it was mostly the influence of the landowning peers and country squires, although the government controlled about thirty seats (**39**). The commercial middle class had relatively little influence. To give some examples: Stamford was controlled by the Cecils, Banbury by Lord North, Boroughbridge by the Duke of Newcastle, Knaresborough by the Duke of Devonshire, Horsham by Viscount Irwin and Lichfield by Earl Gower. A member of the Lambton family sat for Durham City between 1734 and 1813. The smaller the constituency, the more likely it was to be a pocket borough. Some were bought and sold like any other kind of property. In 1761, fifty-one peers had forty-two seats in pocket boroughs and exerted influence over sixty other seats. It was difficult to exert dominant influence over a large electorate, chiefly because of the expense involved. Here political issues could be important. Constituencies like Bristol and Westminster only elected members who would make concessions to the point of view of commercial and trading interests.

George III once remarked, 'This trade of politics is a rascally business. It is a trade for a scoundrel, not for a gentleman.' The ramifications of influence were endless. Sometimes borough patrons did not need to exert any, but merely purchased burgage tenures.

Introduction

County voters had to be sweetened by transporting them at election times, as well as a good deal of wining and dining. Various inducements were offered for borough votes. They included direct money bribes, offers of employment, of tenancies, of government posts, of army or navy contracts for local industries, banquets and gifts to corporations and individuals free drinks in local inns, subscriptions to local hospitals and charities.

Electioneering could be a lively business, especially in large boroughs like Westminster with its 11,000 electors. Here in 1784 the Duchess of Devonshire traded kisses for votes. Bloody brawls between rival factions were commonplace when the flow of free beer inflamed electors. In such boroughs corruption (though it was not regarded as such in the eighteenth century) was not enough. Speeches had to be delivered and manifestoes and handbills produced. However, such constituencies were rare. So long as England was still a predominantly agrarian and rural society, the average elector had little interest in general politics and was willing to leave them to his social betters. This was certainly the case in 1760 and in most places for long afterwards.

Before 1832 the law did not require the keeping of accurate electoral registers. It is therefore difficult to be precise about the size of the electorate. It has been estimated that in 1800 about three adult males in every hundred could vote. In 1831, just before the Reform Act, there were about 435,000 electors in England and Wales, out of a population of 20 million. Even in 1760 the distribution of seats was not geared to the social and economic structure of the country (37). During each subsequent decade the pattern became more anachronistic. Boroughs were concentrated in the south; over half were in Wiltshire and the ten counties bordering the sea south of the Wash and the Severn. Almost a third of English boroughs were seaports, many of which were already sliding into decay by 1760. The five counties of south-west England elected no less than a quarter of the House of Commons. Over 40 per cent of the House was elected by the ten counties south of Bristol and the lower Thames. As late as 1831 Cornwall, with a population of 300,000, sent forty-two members to Westminster. Lancashire, with 1,300,000, sent only fourteen. London was badly underrepresented in proportion to its population. Large towns like Manchester, Birmingham, Leeds and Sheffield, expanding under the impact of the industrial revolution, were unrepresented.

Nevertheless the system worked until the final years of the eighteenth century. By the standards of the time, all major 'interests' were represented in Parliament. Numbers and proportions were regarded as of little consequence. It was property, influence and interests which were important. As Namier has written, eighteenth-century politicians believed in weighing purses, not counting heads.

2 The Problem

The purpose of this book is to examine how and why the representative system of the eighteenth century was transformed into that of the late nineteenth century, a transformation which amounts to a peaceful revolution. About one person in every twenty-four possessed a vote in 1832, about one in twelve in 1867 and one in seven in 1884. The 1884 Reform Act established democracy in principle rather than in practice. As late as 1911 only 29·7 per cent of the total adult population of the United Kingdom were able to vote. Genuine manhood suffrage was delayed until 1918. Viewed from this angle, the evolution towards democracy was very gradual. Yet it was achieved without bloodshed and was a relatively swift process if one bears in mind the entrenched habit of deference among many sections of the population and the powers of survival of the old ruling class (**29, 180, 186, 187**).

During the eighteenth century the system of government and representation had rested on broad social and economic foundations. The landed nobility were still the wealthiest class in the nation. A majority of the population still lived in the countryside and looked to the gentry as the natural leaders of society. Most towns were small by later standards and many were controlled, by one means or another, by local landed magnates (**32** sec. 1). It has been argued that the eighteenth-century electoral system 'worked not unsuccessfully' and, as the political expression of a hierarchical and deferential society, 'could be defended as providing a parliament which reflected the leading interests of the nation and which fulfilled its constitutional role as a check upon the executive power' (**45**). Until 1792 at the earliest, the mass of the people remained unstirred by major political issues.

By the end of the century, however, it was clear that the economic and social infrastructure of the political system was beginning to change. The growth of London as a commercial and industrial centre, as well as the acceleration of industrialisation in the provinces, began to undermine the conception of a carefully graded agricultural community as the microcosm of the nation. New interests were clearly not adequately represented in Parliament. The conflict of 'court versus country' was to be replaced by conflicts between industry and agriculture, between town and countryside, between church and chapel, between labour and capital. The England of Burke was to become the England of Marx.

This process took time. Until at least the turn of the century, political radicalism was largely confined to pre-industrial groups of Dissenters, London artisans and sections of the country gentry. No serious threat was posed to the political power of landed property. By the end of the Napoleonic Wars, the picture had changed. During the early decades of the nineteenth century, it has been wisely pointed out, 'there were, in fact, in Britain two nations struggling in the bosom of one land' (**14,** ch. 1). The old nation was based on the nobility, the gentry, the countryside and the Anglican Church. The new nation rested on industry, commerce, the growing northern and midland towns and the dissenting sects. It was this second nation which provided the rank and file of the parliamentary reform movement and caused it to migrate from London to the northern industrial areas. It was the middle classes of the new nation who created what has been termed the 'entrepreneurial ideal', opposed to the aristocratic ideal (**192,** ch. 8). They wished to see the principles of open competition and the free play of market forces applied to politics and social life as well as to economics. A man should be as free to cast a vote for the political party of his choice as he was to buy and sell goods, to choose a marriage partner or to be a member of a particular religious denomination (**17,** ch. 1). The economics of choice should be accompanied by the politics of choice. Thus patronage and prescription (though not property) were attacked as a brake on the emergence of the liberal state.

The imposition of the Corn Laws in 1815 and the postwar depression brought into the open a struggle between the landed and middle classes which lasted into late Victorian England. In politics, however, the 'triumph of the middle class' was much more restricted than in economics or social life. The 1832 Reform Act preserved enough of the old system to ensure that politics in many places continued to be dominated by the same kind of people as before (**13,** ch. 7). This was especially true at the top. The industrial and commercial classes lacked the leisure and hereditary sources of wealth to enter Parliament sufficiently early to obtain the necessary political experience and training for high office. Hence, as far as parliamentary leadership was concerned, the power of the landed classes lingered on [**doc. 29**]. It could be argued that American corn did more damage to this power than the Reform Acts. The first predominantly middle-class non-landed parliament was elected only in 1906.

There was also the urban working class. Initially composed of the growing bands of skilled craftsmen, artisans, labourers and domestic workers, it came to include factory workers, engineers, miners and railwaymen. The concentration of population in the towns rendered these men conscious of their existence as a class, a consciousness sharpened by the great postwar Reform agitation of 1816–19 (**192**, ch. 6). Many of them shared the eagerness of the middle classes to see changes in the political system and to attack patronage and landed privilege. At the same time they tended to reject the tenets of classical liberalism, extolled by Bentham and the Utilitarians. Their dislike of patronage and dependence was paralleled by their hostility to property rights, *laissez-faire* individualism and the competitive free market. They preferred rather the principle of cooperation and an economic system based on the labour theory of value. These beliefs led to ambivalent working-class attitudes. Sometimes working-class radicals saw the established aristocracy and gentry as their enemy, sometimes the new middle-class 'captains of industry', sometimes (as in the Chartist movement) both at once.

Of course these are simplifications. The social structure of Victorian England was more complex than a crude class model might suggest. Within the landed classes there was often a gulf between the wealthy landlords and the small tenant farmers. Many of the professional middle classes were little more than hangers-on of landed society. Working-class divisions also ran deep, from that between the domestic and factory workers early in the century, to the later one between the skilled and the unskilled. Leaders of the working-class movement were often themselves of middle-class origin, even in the Socialist movement at the end of the century (**178**, ch. 1). The fact remains that the simple class model was held by many contemporaries and was a potent catalyst of political change.

Parliamentary reform, then, was largely a reflection of changes in the economic and social structure of the country. It was one means whereby landed property and patronage was assaulted by middle-class aims of free trade, competition and 'merit' and by working-class ambitions to see the end of the tyranny of property and deference. The problem for historians is largely one of timing. Given the social and economic changes taking place in the nineteenth century, political change was bound to follow. But the actual pace of the coming of democracy was largely dictated by the situation at Westminster. The Bill of 1832 became a possibility only when a period of political crisis at the centre followed the termination of Liverpool's stable government in 1827. The fact that the Tory party split on the Catholic issue enabled the Whigs and Canningites to ally with the Ultras, obtain power, and then retain it by introducing the Reform Bill.

There was a similar situation in 1867. When Palmerston's long period of stable government was brought to an end by his death in 1865, a fissure opened in the Liberal party over the Reform issue. Disraeli was enabled to 'run off with the Whigs' clothes' and push a drastic franchise measure through the House of Commons. The principle of democracy having been admitted in 1867, the Act of 1884 owed even more to cold political calculation. Liberals had long realised the need to broaden the basis of their support in the country-side, especially since the appearance of the new suburban Toryism. But the actual timing of the Act in 1884 was largely the result of the poor record of the Liberal government since 1880 and of Gladstone's desire to do something to placate Chamberlain and the Radicals.

A question which has led to dispute among historians is the influence of extra-parliamentary organisations. The great mass demonstrations of 1831–2 and 1866–7 provided at least a semblance of the threat of revolution. It is impossible to ignore the role of the Birmingham Political Union, the National Union of the Working Classes or the Reform League in making parliamentary reform practical politics. But historians disagree about their significance. Was there a genuine threat of revolution in 1832, which forced the unwilling Whigs to stand by the Bill? Did the Reform League effectively blackmail the government in 1867? Would Reform have come, on both occasions, without such public agitation? Could it not be argued that the second Reform Act came in 1867 because the working class had made it plain after 1848 that they were *not* revolutionary? Despite a good deal of historical research, uncertainty remains.

Economic and social change, the parliamentary situation, the influence of political ideas, the impact of religious Dissent, class ambitions, the role of individuals: each was a factor in the coming of democracy and deserves due consideration.

Part Two

THE TRANSITION TO DEMOCRACY

3 The Early Parliamentary Reform Movement

WILKES AND WYVILL

The mass agitation for parliamentary reform which followed the peace in 1815 had its origins in the earlier Reform movement which dated back to the Wilkes affair of 1763–74. The exclusion of Wilkes from the House of Commons, against the wishes of the Middlesex electors, provoked an explosion of feeling in the Metropolitan area. But if the cry 'Wilkes and Liberty!' opened the door to parliamentary reform, the door did not open very far. Wilkes himself was largely devoid of political ideas. Dissatisfaction with the political system did not lead to coherent doctrines of popular sovereignty and natural rights. The main body of the Wilkites was composed of men 'of the middling sort': merchants, tradesmen, craftsmen, petty traders and lesser freeholders (**46,** ch. 5). Few of them wished to see a genuinely popular democratic electoral system, although some were willing to subscribe to programmes of Reform which included a wider franchise and the abolition of rotten boroughs. What most were worried about was a concentration of power in the hands of the royal executive, an anxiety stemming from seventeenth-century experiences and the writings of John Locke (**45,** ch. 2).

The fall of Pitt in 1761, the 'weak' Peace of Paris in 1763 and the devotion of the King to the despised Bute seemed to signal a phase of more pervasive royal influence and ministerial corruption. Hence the Wilkite demand for the removal of placemen. The affair of Wilkes and No. 45 of the *North Briton* in May 1763, which involved the use of general warrants, seemed confirmation of increasing government tyranny. Pamphlets which appeared before the 1768 election castigated aristocratic government and urged changes in the representative system which would increase the voice of the commercial and manufacturing classes of the London area. A more independent House of Commons, purged of royal and aristocratic influence, would neutralise any attempt at the 'unconstitutional' strengthening of royal power (**45,** ch. 2). Such a House of Commons would be produced by the abolition of rotten boroughs, the removal of placemen and pensioners, annual or triennial parliaments, and, possibly, a wider franchise. Behind these Whiggish sentiments loomed the spectre of class conflict. With few exceptions, Wilkes was opposed by office-holders, clergymen and richer freeholders (**44,** ch. 10). To vote for Wilkes was to vote against the metropolitan social establishment as well as against the government.

A curious alliance between disgruntled political groups, City merchants, lesser freeholders and the London mob, the Wilkites reached their peak in 1774. A subsequent decline was partly a result of their inability to spread their influence beyond the metropolitan area, partly because they became vulnerable to accusations of treachery during the American War. Some of Wilkes's more substantial supporters became alarmed at the involvement of the common people in politics, despite the fact that those at the bottom of the social scale who joined the movement were motivated by high bread prices and hatred of the Scots, rather than dissatisfaction with the political system.

Wilkes, himself no revolutionary, can nevertheless be regarded as the founder of the mass radical movement (**41,** ch. 2). The agitation spread beyond the confines of the City, radical demands for equal representation, annual parliaments and the abolition of rotten boroughs. The activities of the London mob were raised above the traditional level of religious riots, food riots and turbulent strikes. It marked the beginnings of a process, subsequently arrested until 1792, whereby social and economic grievances among the lower classes were directed into political channels.

Despite the fading of the radical agitation, the issues of representation and responsibility remained alive, sustained by the political debate in America and the doctrines of Rousseau and the French *philosophes*. By 1779 defeat in America, unrest in Ireland and the growing burden of taxation revived hostility to the political system. This hostility was focused by the Yorkshire Association of 1780–4, a group of independent country gentlemen led by the Rev Christopher Wyvill. Its activities marked the spread of political radicalism from the metropolitan region to the provinces (**50**). Widespread support was rallied in the country, except amongst those at the bottom of the social ladder. Nationwide county meetings in 1780 were reinforced by links with many of Wilkes's former supporters in Middlesex and the capital. Fox and Burke campaigned in Parliament for the removal of placemen. The petitioning movement rose to a peak (**41**, ch. 3; **45**, ch. 3; **49**).

The aims of the county movement were strictly limited. Wyvill's chief aim was 'economical reform': public economy which would involve the elimination of placemen from the Commons and hence a diminution of royal influence. Economical reform was linked to parliamentary reform, for the executive power could only be effectively restricted by increased county representation and shorter parliaments. However, Wyvill was no modern democrat. It was still land and property that were significant, not numbers. Universal suffrage was best left to the realms of theory.

In any case, the peak of Wyvill's movement was not sustained for long. The Rockingham Whigs cared little for electoral reform other than as a useful political weapon. Many of the discontented country gentlemen were alienated by the extreme radical proposals of the Sub-Committee of the Westminster Association, which included manhood suffrage, annual elections, equal electoral districts, the ballot and payment of M.P.s. The greatest blow to the Association movement was the Gordon Riots of June 1780. Many of those who had supported parliamentary reform now felt that the existing representative system was at least preferable to opening the floodgates of revolution. In fact the common people had little connection with Wyvill's essentially moderate movement. None the less, the Gordon Riots prevented landed and propertied radicals from seeking support from the 'lower orders' for at least a decade.

After 1781 the Association movement declined rapidly. Outside London and Yorkshire there was relatively little support for parliamentary reform. The American crisis, which had stimulated the agitation in the first place, came to an end. Reformers began to quarrel among themselves. When Pitt's Bill for a mild distribution of seats was lost in 1785, the Yorkshire Association wound up. Essentially a revulsion against the 'Court' party and a demand for order and economy in administration, it had little appeal for the masses (**49**). It needed the writings of the English democrats and the outbreak of the French Revolution to root the Reform movement in deeper soil.

JACOBINS AND ENGLISHMEN

In 1788 the Dissenting Societies celebrated the centenary of the 'Glorious Revolution' and linked their demands for civil and religious liberty to those for parliamentary reform (**45,** ch. 6; **52,** introduction). The outbreak of the French Revolution the following year acted as a powerful stimulus to their campaign. Events across the channel were seen as the dawn of European liberty. More dissenting and political clubs sprang up in both London and the provinces. Parliamentary reformers were stimulated by the spectacle of the French nation constructing a constitution from abstract principles, in the light of reason, with little regard for the dead hand of historical precedent. The example of the French seemed to add a new dimension to the struggle for democracy. At first, the Reformers had things very much their own way, since there was little outright hostility to the French Revolution. It could be argued that the French were undergoing a limited constitutional revolution, similar to that of England in the previous century. The traditional concepts of English 'liberty' and French 'slavery' were still potent (**52, 53, 41,** ch. 5; **18,** ch. 10).

The early pattern of response to the French Revolution was broken in late 1790 when Edmund Burke published his *Reflections on the French Revolution*, a book which had enormous influence on the ruling classes of both England and Europe. Burke rejected the doctrine of inherent natural rights as a delusion. Instead, he stressed specific social rights, as an inheritance from the past, based upon reverence for tradition and the existing constitution. Precedent could not be ignored. A new political edifice could rise only from old foundations. The wanton destruction of traditional institutions by the French revolutionaries would bring violence, terror and anarchy, culminating in a military despotism and European war (**20,** chs. 3, 4).

Burke's real target was the English Reformers rather than the French revolutionaries. To the former, it seemed that Burke's arguments could all too easily lend themselves to an inflexible defence of the *status quo*. Burke's *Reflections*, much of which was written in a highly emotional tone, inaugurated an intense debate on the merits of the French Revolution and the necessity for political reform in England. The most famous and influential reply to Burke was Tom Paine's *Rights of Man* (1792). Paine spoke on behalf of the common people, dismissed by Burke as 'the swinish multitude'.

Hereditary rulers and aristocracies were castigated by Paine as a 'banditti of ruffians' who taxed the poor in order to wage wars and line their own pockets. Natural rights mattered more than consitutional rights; the sovereignty of the people must replace that of kings and nobles (**20,** chs. 2, 5; **42,** ch. 4).

By 1792 attitudes towards the French Revolution had changed and opinion polarised. The September Massacres and the creation of the French republic in 1792, the execution of the King and the coming of war with England in 1793: each seemed to confirm Burke's dark prophecy. Even more alarming was the appearance of a 'Jacobin' movement at home, agitating for democracy. The government and the propertied classes were thrown into a panic at the sight of working men demanding political rights. For the Reform movement was no longer confined to Dissenters' 'Constitutional Societies' and 'Revolution Societies', and to organisations like Major Cartwright's Society for Promoting Constitutional Information. Now it seemed that the artisan classes, more or less silent since the days of Wilkes, were breaking the surface again, as a domestic version of the French *menu peuple* or *sans-culottes* (**55,** ch. 1).

Government correspondents in various parts of the country reported popular enthusiasm for the doctrines of Paine. By 1793 over 200,000 copies of the *Rights of Man* had been sold in cheap editions. In Sheffield, over 2500 'lowest mechanics' paraded the dangerous doctrines (**58, 59, 60**). Most alarming of all was the foundation in 1792 of the London Corresponding Society by Thomas Hardy, a shoemaker. Demanding universal suffrage and opposing all privileges, the LCS threw its membership open to all who paid a penny a week and desired manhood suffrage. It served as a bridge between the old Metropolitan radicalism and the new radicalism appearing in the provincial centres, for popular societies modelled on the LCS mushroomed. By March 1792, for example, the Sheffield Constitutional Society had 2000 members, drawn chiefly from the cutlery trades (**55,** ch. 4).

From the moment Revolution broke out across the Channel, members of the Commons were unconvinced by arguments that timely parliamentary reform was the only sure means of avoiding revolution in England. As Windham put it in a Reform debate in 1790: 'What, would he recommend you to repair your house in the hurricane season?' Two years later, the government was churning out anti-Paineite pamphlets and broadsheets and encouraging local gentry and magistrates to organise 'loyal' demonstrations (**50, 57**). Paine himself was outlawed and the *Rights of Man* condemned as a seditious libel. When war broke out in February 1793, a prolonged witch-hunt for 'disloyal' elements was intensified. Booksellers were fined and imprisoned; meetings were broken up; government spies were injected into the bloodstream of the radical movement. In 1793-4 the Scottish reform leaders, after travesties of trials, were given long sentences of transportation. Despite the difficulty of convicting men for political crimes under English law, Pitt moved against the English radical leaders in May 1794. But Hardy and Horne Tooke were acquitted on charges of high treason and escaped the horrors of a traitor's death.

Nevertheless, Pitt's repressive policy brought results. Moderate groups, like the Society for Promoting Constitutional Information and the Society of the Friends of the People, folded up. Even the London Corresponding Society was fatally weakened (**41**, chs. 10-12; **42**, ch. 5). Despite demonstrations in the capital, the 'Two Acts' of 1795 banned political meetings without magistrates' permission and forbad criticism of the monarchy or the government. The leaders of the LCS were arrested and the Society began to disintegrate. Little was left of English liberties; open political meetings and propaganda were now virtually impossible. Intimidation and censorship rendered popular radicalism inarticulate. Small groups of 'Jacobins', who met surreptitiously in London taverns to plot revolution, were flushed out in 1798 (**42**, ch. 5). In an atmosphere of repression, intensified by the naval mutinies of 1797 and the rumblings of rebellion in Ireland, Grey's motion for a Reform Bill was defeated in the House of Commons in May 1797 by 256 to 91 (**41**, chs. 13, 14, **55**, ch. 6).

How far there existed a genuine revolutionary threat in the 1790s, based on keen class antagonism, is debatable. Some historians argue that it was in this crucial decade that a distinct working class consciousness was formed and the liberty tree firmly planted and successfully nourished (**42**, ch. 5, **55**, chs. 4, 6). There is some truth in these arguments. Many of the Reformers active in 1791 and 1792 had been from the propertied classes, including a number of the new industrialists. But the September Massacres and Paineite enthusiasm frightened them into shoring up the political system by joining the landowning ruling class. It may be that if these propertied radicals had been willing to form a lasting union with the popular societies, perhaps supported by discontented elements among the gentry, the government would have been obliged to grant a major instalment of reform. In the event, the brief class alliance of 1792 was not to be repeated until the eve of the 1832 Reform Act.

At the same time, one must beware of exaggerating either the sheer numbers or the class nature of the Reform movement in the 1790s. The latest historian of the rise of modern class society points out that until 1789 parliamentary reform was little more than a Whig cry for reducing the power of the Crown and getting themselves back into office. Even in the peak years of 1792–4 it is doubtful whether either the Society for Promoting Constitutional Information, or the London Corresponding Society, or similar groups in the provinces, succeeded in attracting more than a relatively small minority of their respective classes. The mass loyalty to the established order, manifested at all levels of society, cannot be ignored (**192,** chs. 2, 6). The wind of loyalism which blew across the country in November 1792 flattened a good deal of the reform harvest before it was ripe (**57**).

From 1799 until the end of the war in 1815, it is scarcely possible to speak of a parliamentary reform movement. In Parliament, a small group of Foxite Whigs, including Grey, Romilly and Whitbread, tried to keep the issue alive, although they refused to try to stir a new agitation in the country. Otherwise only Westminster flourished as a centre of Reform activity. Here the radicals, led by Sir Francis Burdett, William Cobbett and Major Cartwright, revived the cause at the 1806 and 1807 elections. It remained alive in London throughout the war years; its leaders were all at the head of the postwar agitation (**61**). On the other hand, the Westminster Committee consisted largely of tradesmen and small masters, rather than the labouring class. Francis Place, the brilliant organiser of the Committee, was especially keen to play down his 'revolutionary' past in the LCS and steer the Committee away from the 'Jacobin' tradition towards a new 'constitutionalist' radicalism, involving a tax-paying franchise and contact with the Benthamites rather than the Paineites.

In the provinces, where repression was harsher and radicals were marked men, there were fewer opportunities for popular radicalism to find an outlet through parliamentary elections. The consequence was a minority conspiratorial movement, expressing itself in secret meetings, illegal trade unionism and Luddism (**42,** chs. 13, 14).

The Transition to Democracy

During the war years, from 1793 to 1815, patriotism tended to reinforce the old society based on dependence, deference and hierarchy, a society which might have otherwise been more seriously modified (**192,** ch. 6). Not even resentment at the commercial policy of the government could shake the basic loyalty of the industrial and commercial classes in the war years. In 1809 Jeremy Bentham wrote his *Plan for Parliamentary Reform* [**doc. 1**]. Here was the new doctrine of Utilitarianism, to be grasped eagerly by those of the middle classes who favoured Reform in order to strengthen their commercial and religious interests, but who refused to accept the Paineite doctrine of natural rights, for fear of encouraging revolution from below. Yet the significant point is that Bentham did not publish the *Plan* until 1817. Only then did the message spread among the middle classes. In his *Plan* and in his *Radicalism Not Dangerous* (1820), Bentham rejected both Burke's appeal to historical prescription and Paine's reliance on the natural rights of man (which Bentham dismissed as 'nonsense on stilts'). Instead he applied the 'utilitarian' test to government and institutions: whether they tended to promote the greatest happiness of the greatest number. Thus Bentham, the real founder of the Liberal tradition, was forced into emphasising the importance of numbers and individuals (**6,** part ii, ch. 5, **22,** part ii).

For the 'greatest happiness' principle to operate, the House of Commons should have an 'identity of interest' with the community. Following his own logic, Bentham came to the conclusion that only manhood suffrage would ensure that the interests of the whole population would be accurately reflected in the legislature. This Utilitarian political philosophy had obvious appeal for those who found Whig doctrines too aristocratic and the concept of the rights of man too revolutionary. When peace came, Utilitarian doctrines spread rapidly among the middle classes, especially when interpreted by James Mill in his *Essay on Government* (1820). Mill savagely attacked the aristocracy as corrupt and inefficient, whilst at the same time judiciously diluting the universal suffrage aspects of Bentham's theory of representation [**doc. 2**].

Thus in 1815 there was no shortage of ideology: Burke for the Tories, Bentham for the new middle classes and Paine for the lower orders. A thriving postwar press—a major factor in the nineteenth century Reform agitation—carried these ideas to wider audiences. Once the war was over, the fetters of dependence were loosened and pent-up resentment at the aristocracy and the pressures of industrialism released. By now, the Industrial Revolution had progressed far enough for a genuine class consciousness to emerge among both masters and workers, especially in Lancashire and Yorkshire. The organised Reform movement in 1816–19 had a wider and sounder base than that of the 1790s. The threat to the power of the landed aristocracy in politics was thus correspondingly greater.

4 The Crisis of Reform

REVIVAL

Peace in 1815 failed to bring prosperity. The loss of wartime markets, the cessation of government contracts, rapid inflation and the demobilisation of the armed services all produced severe depression and discontent, especially in London and the northern textile districts. Popular prints, cartoons, verses and the unstamped press poured scorn on what they regarded as a corrupt political system; corrupt because it channelled wealth to the royal family, placemen, pensioners and fund-holders, while the people starved. Bread riots and demonstrations against high taxation flared in various parts of the country. In the east Midlands there was a revival of Luddism; in East Anglia the savage agrarian riots of 1816 (**62, 65**).

Attempts were soon made to harness the energy released by these spontaneous outbreaks to the parliamentary reform movement. Major Cartwright went back to his original democratic principles and took political radicalism to the Luddite counties on his tours of 1813 and 1815. It was he, more than anyone, who prepared the ground for the postwar reform agitation (**61**). By March 1817, for example, there were forty 'Hampden clubs', inspired by Cartwright, in the Lancashire cotton district. In November 1816 Cobbett found a loophole in the stamp laws and reduced the price of his *Political Register* from 1s 0½d to 2d—the 'Twopenny Trash'. His first cheap number sold 200,000 copies in two months. It urged the people to seek a drastic reform of parliament; to seek it alone if necessary: 'If the *skulkers* will not join you, if the decent fire-side gentry still keep aloof, proceed by yourselves' (**15**, ch. 2, sec. 8, **42**, ch. 16).

A month later, it became clear that the people would have to proceed by themselves. The Spa Fields Riots of December 1816 involved the Spenceans and insurrectionary elements among the Jacobins of the London tavern world. They emitted a whiff of revolution and frightened middle-class reformers away from the popular radical movement at the very outset of the postwar agitation. With few exceptions, provincial manufacturers and merchants remained hostile to the powerful mass radical movement (**42,** ch. 15).

Not that the new propertied middle classes regarded the existing political system as satisfactory. In 1815 the *Leeds Mercury* wrote: 'There can be no equity in the landed interest forming nine-tenths, at least, of our representatives; while the commercial and trading interest, which is equal in magnitude and importance, is sunk into insignificance.' During the later stages of the war, many of the northern industrial leaders had expressed their dissatisfaction with the commercial and financial policy of the government. In 1812 they had mounted a successful campaign for the repeal of the Orders in Council, which had caused the USA to close its markets to British exports. This victory for middle-class opinion was consolidated in the following year, when the East India Company's monopoly of the Indian trade (though not the Chinese trade) was abolished. There still, however, remained Pitt's income tax, which seemed an example of the unequal distribution of the burden of war finance between the owners of land and the owners of capital. Equally disliked were the duties imposed on imported raw cotton and wool (**15,** ch. 3, sec. 6).

These issues seemed to underline the fact that the interests of landed society and those of the new industrial urban society were increasingly divergent. During the war, with the French Revolution and the English Jacobins so fresh in the memory, the middle classes had been unwilling to press hard for changes in the electoral system; an attitude stiffened by the Luddite risings of 1812.

However, peace in 1815 failed to remove serious grievances. The depression which brought unemployment to the workers also cut manufacturers' profits and provoked intense competition. Inflation eroded both capital and credit. Heavy war-time taxation was retained, although middle-class pressure helped to remove the income tax in 1816. The cotton and wool duties were not repealed, while the Corn Law of 1815 drew strong protests from manufacturers and merchants, who argued that it injured industry without aiding agriculture. The sight of a landed parliament seeking to look after its own was intensely irritating to industrial and commercial interests. Yet despite their grievances, voiced in the provincial press, the middle classes were pushed over to the side of law and order and government, by the mass agitation after 1815 (**63,** ch. 4).

Thus the ground was cleared for a straight fight between the government and popular radicalism; although the latter had some sympathisers among the intelligentsia, for example Byron, Shelley, Hazlitt and Leigh Hunt's *Examiner*. Radical newspapers like Cobbett's *Political Register*, Wooler's *Black Dwarf*, Richard Carlile's *Republican* and Wade's *Gorgon* raged against the corrupt rule of landowners, placemen and fundholders. Henry 'Orator' Hunt thundered from radical platforms. The Spa Fields riots of 1816 were followed by the pathetic 'March of the Blanketeers' in Manchester in March 1817 and the Pentridge Revolution in June in South Derbyshire, for which Jeremiah Brandreth went to the scaffold (**62**, ch. 14). As in 1794, the government's response was repression. Once again Habeas Corpus was suspended. The Seditious Meetings Act suppressed many reform clubs and societies. Government spies were ubiquitous and arrests were frequent [**doc. 3**].

After a trade revival in 1818, depression returned again the following year. Once more northern workers turned to political demonstrations; this time with little help from a fragmented and weak London radicalism. Mass meetings and the press were employed to reach the thousands of operatives who were not already members of political clubs. Demonstrations at Birmingham and Leeds [**doc. 4**] were followed by the 'Peterloo Massacre' of August 1819 in Manchester, when the yeomen charged a peaceful crowd which had gathered to hear Hunt castigate the government. Eleven were killed and over four hundred injured (**64**). Despite protests from the radicals, including many of the middle class, the government congratulated the Manchester magistrates and rejected demands for an inquiry. The Six Acts were passed to stifle the radical press and prevent mass meetings (**68**).

In 1820 trade improved and the provincial mass radical movement died away. In London, the decline was hastened by the fiasco of the Cato Street conspiracy and the distraction of the trial of Queen Caroline (**42**, ch. 15). Throughout the country, general prosperity between 1820 and 1825 brought falling prices and more employment. The whole decade was relatively calm; working men tended to turn to Owenism, trade unionism, self-education and the agitation for a free unstamped press. In 1824 Wooler abandoned the *Black Dwarf*, lamenting that there was now no 'public devotedly attached to the cause of parliamentary reform' (**72**).

BROKEN WHIGS AND OUTRAGED ULTRAS

Prospects for reform now looked bleak. Pressure from some middle-class groups, led by Edward Baines, editor of the *Leeds Mercury*, for the transference of rotten borough seats to new industrial towns had very limited results [**doc. 5**]. In 1821 Grampound (Cornwall) was disfranchised and its seats given to Yorkshire, though not to Leeds as the reformers had hoped. Even this was regarded by Lord Eldon as a step into 'the whirlpool of democracy'. In 1828 Penryn and East Retford, notoriously corrupt boroughs, lost their seats. But the House of Lords refused to allow those of Penryn to be transferred to Manchester. Apart from these minor changes, the representative system remained the same as it had been in 1707, apart from the addition of the hundred Irish members in 1800 as a result of the Act of Union.

Until 1827 Liverpool's government was firmly entrenched in power, consolidated by the admission of Peel, Canning and Huskisson after 1821. Although manufacturers and merchants welcomed Huskisson's limited free trade measures and Canning's liberal foreign policy, the 'Liberal Tories' made no serious moves towards parliamentary reform. Indeed, Canning denied that Reform 'would enable the House to discharge its functions more usefully than it discharges them at present'.

The Whig opposition had been regarded as the party of Reform since the days of Fox, although they had never in fact adopted it as party policy. It seemed unlikely that they would gain power. The *émeutes* of 1817 and 1819 had panicked the hundred or so 'waverers' in the Commons; they were sometimes willing to support the Whigs on specific issues, but consistently blocked attempts to bring down the government (**69,** chs. 5–7). Moreover, the 'enlightened Tory' regime of 1824–7 made the running and reduced the Whigs to tacitly supporting liberal elements in the government. In 1827 Whig fortunes reached their nadir and the party seemed in danger of dissolution

When Liverpool resigned, some Whigs joined Canning's administration, but only in subordinate positions. After Canning's death, the mediocre Goderich ministry came and went, while the union between Whigs and liberal Tories was dissolved. In 1828 Wellington formed a Tory ministry, but soon lost the support of the 'Canningites' on the left wing of the party. He and Peel then proceeded to alienate the right wing in 1829 by passing Catholic emancipation. These political manoeuvres were of crucial importance, for the ruling class became seriously divided. A consequence was that parliamentary reform began to be seen as a useful weapon in political tactics (**69**, chs. 9, 10; **73**, ch. 9).

The Catholic Relief Act was the last straw for many 'Ultra' peers and country squires. They went into opposition and left the Wellington ministry dangerously weak. Their dislike of the 'liberal Tories', whom they regarded as prisoners of the new 'economists', had been intensified by government deflationary policy. The 'Country Party' saw this policy as a root cause of agricultural depression. Relaxation of the Corn Law in 1828 seemed a further blow to agrarian interests. So dissatisfied were the Ultras, that they were even prepared to countenance parliamentary reform. Reform was to be employed, not as a means of furthering democratic principles, but in order to reduce the power of ministers by striking at nomination boroughs, seen as a major source of ministerial power. Thus Catholic emancipation marked the initial stage of the reform crisis (**77**).

The next stage came in 1830, when a sudden slump in the economy brought widespread distress in both industry and agriculture. Rebates of agrarian rents were frequent; unemployment in the manufacturing districts increased. Revolution in France helped to raise the political temperature. Radical reform demonstrations appeared once more. In January, Thomas Attwood founded the influential Birmingham. Political Union, while similar unions were established in both London and the provinces (**74**, ch. 2). Cobbett toured the country and called loudly for Reform in the columns of the *Political Register*.

In the past, such troubled times had caused a Tory government to serve as a rallying point for those anxious to preserve law and order. But Wellington's government was now too weak to fulfil this function. In any case there was probably less fear of Reform than ten years earlier. The long absence of strident agitation, plus the opinions of the Benthamites (put forward in the *Westminster Review*), had combined to make reform more respectable.

Moreover, the Ultras felt that Wellington's government was incapable of alleviating the prevailing distress. The Ultra solution was protection and currency reform, both of which figured prominently at a series of county meetings in 1829 (**77**). Wellington survived an Ultra amendment to the Address in February 1830 only with the support of Whigs and Liberals anxious to defend an administration which had passed Catholic emancipation. The death of George IV in the summer necessitated a general election. Already some Whigs, like Russell, were arguing that reasonable concessions on parliamentary reform were the answer to a potentially revolutionary situation. Antiministerial Tories emphasised the need for protection, currency reform and parliamentary reform in order to remove distress, reduce ministerial power and strengthen the 'independent' landed interest.

A large number of new members were returned at the election. Most of them were hostile to the ministry and many were pledged to parliamentary reform. In this situation, with reform feeling spreading rapidly, the Whigs swiftly reunited. Agreement was reached with the Ultras and the Canningites. Brougham, flushed with his victory at the Yorkshire election, persuaded the Whig leaders to accept a plan of moderate Reform. Meanwhile, Wellington's bid for Canningite support failed. In the country, anxiety was increased by the outbreak of the 'Swing' riots in the southern and eastern agrarian counties (**79, 81**).

When Parliament reassembled in November 1830, Wellington made a last desperate bid for Ultra support by uttering an uncompromising denial of the need for parliamentary reform. It proved vain, since most of the Country Party were convinced that Grey and the Whigs were more likely to introduce measures dealing with agrarian distress. Largely because of the hostility of the Ultras and the new members, the ministry was defeated on a civil list vote. Rather than face Brougham's forced debate on parliamentary reform, Wellington somewhat precipitately resigned. William IV immediately sent for Grey, who formed a coalition under Whig leadership. Back in power for the first time since 1806, the Whigs saw their initial task as the introduction of a Reform Bill (**74,** ch. 2; **69,** ch. 10).

THE WHIG RECIPE

Grey and most of his colleagues were thoroughbred aristocrats, with little sympathy for radical democratic principles. Trade unions were regarded as seditious; extra-parliamentary political organisations were distrusted; most members of the government heartily approved of the draconian sentences meted out to the 'Swing' rioters. At the same time, there was some variation of opinion within the government. Durham, Brougham and Russell were keen reformers: Melbourne and Palmerston, on the other hand, could rarely summon up enthusiasm for the question: Stanley and Lansdowne were non-committal.

Whilst Grey was no democrat, he was an old reformer, willing to accept reasonable political innovation. Circumstances in 1830 revived his interest in reform, an interest which had cooled considerably since the days he had stood with Fox in the 1790s. Distress, the growth of public opinion, revolution on the continent, apparent changes in the social structure: all combined to push Grey towards reform. So did his unwillingness to see the Whigs return to the political wilderness they had so long inhabited.

Close contact with his son-in-law, Durham ('Radical Jack'), and his son, Hawick, plus the propaganda of James Mill and the Utilitarians, made Grey conscious of the importance of the new provincial merchanting and manufacturing classes. He wrote of them as those 'who have made wonderful advances in both property and intelligence'. Such was the demand for reform that Grey became convinced that some concession would have to be made. As he informed the king: 'With the universal feeling that prevails on this subject, it is impossible to avoid doing something; and not to do enough to satisfy public expectation (I mean the satisfaction of the rational public) would be worse than to do nothing.'

Thus the Whig recipe for avoiding revolution was to be concession; as Macaulay urged, 'Reform that you may preserve' [**doc. 7**]. In a renewed climate of distress and discontent, traditional Whig doctrines of government by consent and resistance to oppression made it difficult to adopt a deliberately repressive policy. Whigs had a good deal of respect for public opinion, as expressed in meetings, petitions and journals. Above all, they wished to avoid violence and to smooth the path to peaceful change. Their theory of representation impelled them to enfranchise the new industrial towns and get rid of the worst rotten boroughs. These old arguments were reinforced by a new one: that reform be used as a means of alleviating distress and avoiding revolution. The threat of revolution seemed real enough to many, even in late 1830. An anonymous letter received by the government warned: 'Depend upon it the country is ripe for revolution . . . then goodbye to England's King and Ministers!' (**74**, ch. 4).

There were frequent appeals to history. Durham argued that the French Revolution and the loss of the American colonies could both have been forestalled by timely concessions. According to Macaulay, revolutions occurred when social and economic change outpaced political change. Hence the need to attach the middle classes to the existing system, which tended to push 'over to the side of revolution those whom we shut out from power. Is this a time when the cause of law and order can spare one of its natural allies?' A revolutionary alliance between the middle classes and the lower orders would destroy the constitution, either now or in the near future. Macaulay played on such fears in a Commons debate on the Reform Bill in March 1831:

> The danger is terrible. The time is short. If this bill should be rejected, I pray to God that none of those who concur in rejecting it may ever remember their votes with unavailing remorse, amidst the wreck of laws, the confusion of ranks, the spoliation of property and the dissolution of the social order [**doc. 7**].

The essence of the Whig case was that the power and prestige of government would become increasingly ineffective and dependent on mere coercion, unless legitimised by the consent of 'respectable' public opinion. Reform would re-establish the legitimacy of the political system by attaching to it, to quote Mackintosh, 'all persons who have risen in wealth, in intelligence, in any of the legitimate sources of ascendancy over others'.

In the autumn of 1830 Grey appointed a committee of four (Russell, Durham, Duncannon and Graham) and instructed it 'that the outline of a measure be prepared, large enough to satisfy public opinion and afford sure ground of resistance to further innovation', but at the same time 'maintaining the essential character of the Constitution'. The result of the committee's secret deliberations were revealed when Russell introduced the first Reform Bill in the House of Commons on 1 March 1831. The Bill planned to disfranchise many small boroughs with tiny populations, often nomination boroughs under the control of a patron. Some other boroughs, with slightly larger populations, were to lose one of their two members. A number of these seats were to be given to hitherto unrepresented boroughs; still more were to go to the counties. A few were given to Wales, Scotland and Ireland. The county franchise was to remain with the 40s freeholders, but the borough vote was made uniform:

the occupation of buildings, as owner or tenant, worth an annual value of £10 (**74,** ch. 5).

If the Whig response to the threat of revolution was to be concession, then they were careful not to concede more than was absolutely necessary. The attention of contemporaries, and of historians, concentrated on the enfranchisement of the new boroughs and the £10 householder vote. This has conveyed a misleading impression and made the Bill seem more radical than it actually was, as no doubt the Whigs intended. The recent researches of Professor Gash and Professor Moore have shown that the Act was essentially conservative; so much so that Professor Moore is sceptical about the whole concept of 'concession' (**86, 87, 77, 78, 93**). If the Whigs wished to broaden slightly the basis of political power, it is also true that they had no intention of undermining the essential control of the system by the landed aristocracy and gentry [**doc. 9**]. Grey spoke honestly in the House of Lords in September 1831: 'I am indeed convinced that the more the Bill is considered, the less it will be found to prejudice the real interests of the aristocracy.'

Certainly the Whigs had no intention of introducing anything smacking of genuine democracy. In November 1831 Grey declared: 'There is no one more decided against annual parliaments, universal suffrage and the ballot, than I am. My object is not to favour, but to put an end to such hopes and projects.' The aim was to attach to the constitution the 'middle classes', eulogised by many politicians, by newspapers like the *Manchester Guardian* and the *Leeds Mercury*, and by commentators like James Mill [**doc. 2**]. Grey himself had referred to 'the middle classes . . . who form the real and efficient mass of public opinion and without whom the power of the gentry is nothing'.

Yet these middle classes were hard to define. Indeed, in 1832 they constituted something of a social myth. They were certainly not a widespread and coherent social group, with a unified political outlook. Influential in the new industrial towns, they were not dominant in more than a very few parts of the country. Major areas of English society were still essentially preindustrial, and were to remain so after 1832 (**88,** introduction). The £10 borough franchise included a wide variety of occupation groups, many of which had contrary interests. It is unlikely that the Whigs were thinking primarily in economic terms. The key word that cropped up continually was 'respectable'. The franchise must not be given to those who would use it 'irresponsibly'—those who lacked respectability and some degree of deference to the existing constitution and to a political system based on the divine right of property (**91**).

'Respectability', with its inevitable moral connotations, was equated exclusively (and falsely) with the new industrial and commercial leaders; with shopkeepers and professional men. The concept seemed to have little relevance to those whose lot it was to labour, as viewed through the eyes of the propertied classes. Property was held to be the only satisfactory yardstick of 'respectability' and 'responsibility'. Thus the traditional basic qualification for political rights was to be retained. Landed wealth would be augmented by commercial and industrial wealth.

A survey conducted in Leeds by Edward Baines convinced Russell of the soundness of his choice of a £10 property qualification for the borough franchise [**doc. 6**]. He was soothingly assured that the £10 qualification in Leeds 'did not admit to the exercise of the elective franchise a single person who might not safely and wisely be enfranchised'. When Russell attempted to include the ballot and shorter parliaments in the Bill, he was obliged to raise the franchise qualification to £20 in order to pacify the Cabinet. However, voting by secret ballot was regarded as furtive and somehow 'un-English', whilst it was widely felt that shorter parliaments would impede the tasks of government. Accordingly, both Russell's proposals were eventually rejected and the £10 qualification restored. It answered the Whigs' purpose, for it included those merchanting and manufacturing groups which felt that their interests at Westminster were not properly represented by the county members or a resort to petitioning (**70**). Hence the giving of seats to towns like Manchester, Birmingham, Leeds and Bradford.

Examination of some of the other clauses of the Bill serves to underline the conservative intentions of the Whig Cabinet. First, the £10 qualification was closely hedged by ratepaying, registration and residence clauses, which considerably narrowed the range of its operation. Secondly, there was a subtle attempt to preserve the influence of the landed interest and cushion the effects of the concession made to the middle classes. Boroughs were not enfranchised according to a rigid Benthamite calculus of wealth and population. Russell disclaimed any desire to produce uniformity; on the contrary, he stressed the need to ensure that a mass of interests, great and small, were adequately represented.

Thus Frome, with a relatively small population, was given seats because its woollen industry would represent that of the south-west and help to balance that of the mighty West Riding. Whitby and Sunderland, both small towns, were given seats in order to enlarge the shipping interest. A hundred seats were reserved for places with no specific economic interests and hence 'better qualified to speak and inform the House on great questions of general interest to the community'.

The Whigs had no objection to 'legitimate' influence, exercised in the country village by the squire, or in the industrial borough by the millowner. Nomination boroughs were thinned out, since influence was exercised 'illegitimately' in them, because of small populations and the frequent non-residence of patrons. Burgage boroughs were not regarded as genuine communities, because their voters were usually few and non-resident. Throughout the Reform Bill debates, the Whigs studiously pointed out their desire to create genuine political communities, where influence would be legitimised by residence (voters had to live within a seven-mile radius of the borough) and a reasonably large population (**77**).

The Whigs shared the anxiety of the landed interest at the growing influence in the counties of urban voters. Particularly striking examples were the influence of Birmingham residents in the Warwickshire county elections, of Manchester men in Lancashire and of Leeds and Bradford residents in Yorkshire. It seemed as though this growing influence might result in the erosion of landed control of the county seats. In the first Reform Bill, the Whigs took steps to prevent such quarrels among the propertied classes at election time. The gentry were protected by disqualifying borough electors from voting in counties. Boundary changes were also employed in the attempt to insulate industrial interests from those of the landed gentry and thus prevent the two clashing at elections. More seats for the counties were an additional safeguard.

DEBATE

Opponents of the Bill were not convinced by Grey's claim that the government was defending 'the real interests of the aristocracy'. As controversy began to centre upon the £10 borough franchise and the abolition of nomination boroughs, so the conservative nature of the

Bill tended to be overlooked. Moreover, the agitation outside Parliament frightened many members and exaggerated the forebodings of anti-reformers. The introduction of the first Reform Bill in March 1831 opened a debate which, in the words of Professor Gash, 'went to the roots of political philosophy'. The Tories, by this time healing their previous divisions and rapidly uniting against reform, argued that the Bill would destroy the old 'balance of the constitution', consecrated by Blackstone and sanctified by Burke. The influence of the crown, diminished since 1760 by economical reform and restriction of patronage, would suffer a further decline. The freedom of the monarch to choose his ministers would be inhibited by fear of antagonising public opinion, henceforward to be channelled through a reformed House of Commons. The loss of rotten boroughs would make the task of government more difficult, since it would not be so easy for unpopular ministers, rejected by ignorant voters, to find safe seats. Similarly, the power of the House of Lords would decline as that of the Commons increased. The final result would be the absence of checks on the will of the popular assembly, itself little more than the passive instrument of a fickle public opinion (**86,** ch. 1) [**doc. 8**].

Neither were the Tories reassured by the Whig attempt to separate rural and agrarian constituencies. Instead of viewing it as a bid to strengthen the landed interest at a time of inevitable political change, they argued that it would lead to a clash of economic interests. In Parliament at least, industry would be ranged against agriculture, with the former an odds-on favourite. Already, it was noticed, reform petitions from Manchester demanded the repeal of the Corn Laws.

The abolition of small boroughs, and the loss of certain franchises was regarded by anti-reformers as a 'revolutionary' seizure of private property without compensation, as well as a ruthless setting aside of customary rights. Such a dangerous precedent, it was argued, could well lead to attacks on other kinds of property. The final argument of the opponents of the Bill was that, however moderate the Whigs claimed the measure to be, it was the thin end of the democratic wedge. 'I was unwilling', declared Peel later, 'to open a door which I saw no prospect of being able to close'.

Once the constitution had been changed, under pressure of public demand, then more drastic changes could be made in the near future. Such changes, argued Peel, would inevitably culminate in democracy, still a perjorative term on both sides of the House in 1831–2. Power would pass to Burke's 'swinish multitude': uneducated, unprincipled, immoral, selfish and grasping. The old ideal of disinterested and efficient aristocratic government would be gone for ever [**doc. 8**].

The Whigs themselves appreciated some of these arguments. After all, Burke was a Whig philosopher and they too subscribed to the ideal of an aristocratic government and a balanced constitution. When obliged to ask the king to create enough peers to overcome the resistance of the House of Lords, Grey did so with obvious reluctance and distaste. Russell reserved some nomination boroughs in the Bill for use as safe ministerial seats.

Nevertheless the Whigs stood by their initial argument: that the existing system was unsatisfactory, in that it left important interests unrepresented and was widely regarded as neither disinterested nor efficient. Those new interests had to be attached to the constitution, to the side of law and order, before the threat of revolution became reality [**doc. 7**]. Some of these arguments were accepted by a number of Tories who, looking back to Catholic emancipation in 1829, realised that the party in power could not afford to remain on the high horse of constitutional theory and gaze far into the distant future. The first task of the government was to govern, which meant a necessary preoccupation with present circumstances. Thus the fundamental case of the ministry was that, unless a genuine Reform Bill were passed, its task would become impossible.

THE PROGRESS OF THE BILL

The various arguments for and against reform were put forward in an atmosphere of intense political crisis, which lasted for over a year. The second reading of the Bill passed by a single vote on 22 March, but soon afterwards the Tories passed an amendment objecting to a reduction in the total number of MPs. Grey decided to appeal to the people, or to be more exact, to the unreformed electorate. The king was persuaded to grant a dissolution. Public opinion, in the shape of the electorates of large 'open' boroughs and the counties, declared for reform at the general election of April 1831. Seventy-six of the eighty-two county members supported the Bill.

The opposition did all it could to delay the Reform Bill in committee. It succeeded in inserting the 'Chandos clause'. This gave county votes to tenants-at-will paying £50 a year—farmers who would be little more than political serfs of their landlords (**93**). The government's answer to this was to permit more urban penetration of the counties in order to neutralise the 'illegitimate' influence of landlords over the tenant farmers. Borough freeholders could now vote in counties if their borough property failed to qualify them for the borough franchise. On 22 September the third reading of the Bill passed by 109 votes. It then went up to the Lords (**74**, ch. 7).

After a five-night debate, the Lords threw out the Bill by forty-one votes, twenty-one of which came from the bench of bishops. 'The bishops have done it,' wrote the 'infidel' Carlile sarcastically, 'it is the work of the Holy Ghost'. Petitions from various parts of the country had warned the Lords against defying the will of the people. There now followed an explosion of fury against the peers. Radical newspapers appeared with the black edges of mourning; mass meetings were organised by the political unions; the Duke of Newcastle, a notorious boroughmonger, was mobbed; the windows of Apsley House, home of the Duke of Wellington, were smashed; there were serious riots at Nottingham and Derby; at Bristol the mob ran riot for two days.

Grey was now left with two alternatives: either to persuade the king to declare willingness to create sufficient peers to overcome the resistance of the Lords, or to make changes in the Bill to attract the waverers in the upper House. The refusal of the king made the first course impossible; so the second was adopted. The third, revised, Reform Bill was introduced by Russell on 12 December. The £10 borough qualification was simplified. A number of boroughs scheduled to lose one of their two members were reprieved. Resident freemen were to retain their borough votes. The second reading was carried by 324 to 162, exactly two to one.

Although the king hinted in January 1832 that he might prove willing to create peers, Grey was reluctant to ask him to do so unless absolutely necessary. The demands of Althorp and Durham for immediate action were rejected. Meanwhile, the Bill went drearily through the committee stage and passed its third reading in the Commons on 22 March. Grey's patience proved justified, for by now the waverer group had been augmented and on 13 April the peers passed the second reading by 184 to 175.

The crisis suddenly blew up again when the Tories passed an

amendment seeking to postpone discussion of the disfranchisement clauses in committee. The opposition leaders had made the error of assuming that Grey would neither resign nor seek the creation of Whig peers over such a minor issue. But the prime minister regarded it as an unconstitutional attempt to dictate terms to the government. He asked the king to create peers. But William IV's attitude had stiffened since Christmas, largely because of the hostility of his domestic advisers to the Bill, but also because of his dislike of the agitation in the country. On 14 April he refused to create fifty new peers and accepted the resignation of the Grey government.

The consequence was the 'days of May', a wave of protests and demonstrations, when London radicals did all they could to prevent the creation of a Tory administration. Wellington tried to form a government, even though it would entail the introduction of a Reform Bill. The attempt was nullified by Peel's refusal to join on such terms. For the king there was now no escape. He was obliged to send for Grey and agree to the creation of sufficient peers to quell all opposition in the Lords. The threat proved enough. Informed of the king's decision, the upper House allowed the Reform Bill through the committee stage within a few days. On 4 June it was read for the third time by 106 to 22. Three days later it received the royal assent, although William spitefully refused to do so in person. The Bill was now the great Reform Act of 1832 and the Reform crisis was over [**doc. 11a**]..

REVOLUTION AVOIDED?

Nineteenth-century historians argued that a revolutionary situation existed in 1831–2 and that an outbreak was averted only by timely concessions in the shape of the passing of the Reform Act. Modern historians writing in the Whig tradition, including G. M. Trevelyan and J. R. M. Butler, have taken a similar view, which has found its way into the textbooks. So have recent left-wing historians. E. P. Thompson argues that 'in the autumn of 1831 and in the "days of May" Britain was within an ace of revolution', a revolution akin to those of 1848 in Europe and the Paris Commune of 1871 (**42**, ch. 16). E. J. Hobsbawm has written of 'something like a revolutionary situation' in 1831–2 (*The Age of Revolution*, Weidenfeld and Nicolson, 1962).

Without doubt, some of the ingredients of revolution were present. Among them were economic distress, unrest among both industrial and agricultural workers, the influence of the July Revolution in Paris and signs of a serious division among the ruling class. There was also a well-organised radical movement, including organisations like the Birmingham Political Union, the National (i.e. London) Political Union and the National Union of the Working Classes. Neither can it be denied that widespread support existed in the country for the government and the Reform Bill [**doc. 10**]. The opponents of the Bill were never able to mount a major agitation against Reform; their meetings and petitions were pretty rare and represented relatively few. They proved incapable of organising anything like the mass meetings in Birmingham in October 1831 and May 1832, arranged by the BPU, according to its leaders 'the Barometer of the Reform feeling throughout the kingdom'.

Moreover, the Reform crisis was regularly punctuated by violence. There were riots at the London demonstrations of April and October 1831. The general election of that year was accompanied by rioting in Scotland. After the peers rejected the second Bill in October 1831, there were serious outbreaks of violence at Derby, Nottingham and Bristol. In the 'days of May' of 1832 there was the famous run on gold, as well as talk of the collection of arms, of a revolutionary march on London, of the non-payment of taxes, of disaffection in the army.

Non-political violence also aggravated feelings of insecurity at a time when the forces of public order were weak and memories of the French Revolution were strong. Important manifestations of this kind of violence were a renewed outbreak late in 1831 of the rural arson and machine-breaking of late 1830 and violent strikes in the mining areas of Northumberland, Durham, Staffordshire and Wales (**81**). There is evidence of alarm among the ruling classes. J. C. Hobhouse, a radical MP and later a Whig minister, wrote in his 1832 diary that many of the aristocracy 'believe themselves, and perhaps are, on the brink of destruction'.

Recently, however, a brilliant book by a Yale political scientist has thrown doubt on the traditional concept of the 'threat of revolution' in 1830–2 (**83**). Professor Hamburger demonstrates how the ingredients of revolution were made to seem more potent than they really were by a strong dash of rhetoric, added by James Mill and the Benthamite radicals. Mill believed that the aristocracy would never concede power voluntarily, but only from motives of calculated self-interest. Whilst they would, no doubt, surrender to violence, Mill himself had no wish to see any fundamental challenge to the social order. He believed that the government would also give way before the *threat* of revolution.

Accordingly, he advocated a kind of political brinkmanship, whereby Benthamite radicals would do all in their power to convey to the government an image of an impatient, threatening public opinion, ready to plunge the country into revolution if its demands were not met. The passing of a 'genuine' Reform Bill would meet the demands and relieve the pressure. Mill transmitted his ideas to influential radicals like Francis Place and Joseph Parkes. Place was the *éminence grise* behind the London Political Union, while Parkes was prominent in the Birmingham Political Union, as well as feeding *The Times* and the *Morning Chronicle* with news reports of Reform meetings and demonstrations (**83,** ch. 2).

Place, Parkes and their associates did all they could to implement Mill's doctrine of the 'language of menace'. Press reports, petitions and public demonstrations were designed to emphasise the depth of reform feeling and to persuade the government of the inevitability of revolution unless it kept its nerve and stood by its Reform Bill. The Millite radicals were in a strong position to influence the government. Ministers were impressed by the size and organisation of the Birmingham Political Union (**80**). Place was regarded, especially by Melbourne, as a reliáble source for the current state of public feeling. Hobhouse was in close touch with both the Benthamite radicals and the administration. Mill and Brougham were friends. Furthermore, ministers relied constantly on the press for information about the state of public opinion. But such information was usually obtained by the newspapers and journals from Benthamite radical sources.

By means of news reports, BPU and NPU bills and placards, and deputations to the ministry, Place and Parkes hammered home their message. Its essence was that Reform feeling in the country was so intense that it was held back from the verge of revolution only by the strength of political union organisation and the willingness of the Whig leaders to push through the Reform Bill (**83,** ch. 3).

There was, of course, another side to the coin, insufficiently stressed by Hamburger. The government was not a mere puppet, manipulated by Benthamite strings. Grey initially believed that the

Reform Bill would pass without the need either to seek a dissolution or the creation of peers. When these beliefs proved false, he was in no position to backtrack on the government's promise of half a million extra votes. Only a vast agitation would allow the promise to be kept. Hence Grey resisted pressure for legal action against the political unions, which can be regarded almost as allies of the government (**80**). Ministers could scarcely have been displeased with the image, admittedly largely created by Place and Parkes, of a public opinion so solidly behind the Reform Bill [**doc. 10**]. Between November 1830 and March 1831, there were over six hundred petitions to Parliament for the Reform Bill.

The fact remains that much of what the Benthamites said and did was calculated to mislead and owed more to rhetoric than reality. One of the group, J. A. Roebuck, wrote in 1848 that 'to attain our end, much was said that no one really believed'. The private correspondence of Place and Parkes reveals the dichotomy between the image and the reality of the threat of revolution. They admitted that Reform feeling was never as strong as they claimed in public. When it fell off, for example after October 1831, they privately stressed the need to ginger it up. Until December 1831 the National Political Union had only 6000 members, although a further 14,000 were to join before the Reform crisis was over. Attendances were constantly exaggerated in the press. Figures of 150–200,000 quoted for the two Birmingham meetings exceeded the total population of the city and its environs. It is doubtful whether more than 40,000 could have stood on Newhall Hill, the site of the great outdoor meetings. In any case, BPU leaders laid stress on the peaceful disposition of the crowds and discounted feverish excitement or revolutionary fervour (**83**, ch. 4).

The peak of Millite radical influence was in the 'days of May' 1832, when they strove their utmost to prevent the formation of a Tory administration. Supposing Wellington had formed a government? Place later assured Hobhouse 'there would, positively, have been a rising if Wellington had recovered power'. Although the situation never occurred, there is no real evidence that the radicals intended to stimulate and lead genuine revolution. They neither attempted to seduce the army from its loyalty, nor tried to collect arms and create a national revolutionary organisation. It is extremely unlikely that Place, Parkes and their colleagues possessed the authority necessary to summon up a national rising.

Their chief preoccupation was always with the image of revolution and with their role as a sustained pressure group on the Whig ministry. In the event, the final agitation was largely confined to London and was financial in character. Place's inspired slogan, 'To stop the Duke, go for Gold', helped to drain the Bank of England of forty per cent of its gold reserves. How far the conversions were owing to political motives, and how far to social and financial panic, is hard to tell. For all the rumours of a 'march on London', the provinces remained relatively calm.

When they constantly emphasised the unanimity and class harmony of reformers, the Benthamite radicals recognised a major weakness in their image of imminent insurrection. Place took elaborate steps to minimise the impact of disharmony. Hence the mass meetings, where conditions made it difficult for manhood suffrage radicals to pass hostile amendments. Place did all he could to exclude 'extremists' from the Council of the National Political Union. Melbourne was persuaded to ban demonstrations by the National Union of the Working Classes, thus leaving the NPU supreme in London. But fissures in the Reform movement could not be completely disguised or brushed aside as insignificant.

The radicals who met at the Blackfriars Rotunda and created the National Union of the Working Classes regarded Place as a traitor to his class and the Reform Bill as an irrelevant middle-class nostrum (**42,** ch. 16). Men like Carlile, Hetherington, Watson, Cleave and Lovett wanted universal suffrage, the ballot, annual parliaments, a free unstamped press and a denial of the equation between political rights and property rights (**105,** chs. 3, 4). The *Poor Man's Guardian* argued that the supporters of the Reform Bill did not wish to undermine or remodel aristocratic institutions, 'but to consolidate them by a reinforcement of sub-aristocracy from among the middle classes' [**doc. 11b**]. Nevertheless, the Rotunda radicals, mostly artisans, proved unable to unite behind them the disorganised and varied masses of London's unskilled labourers. Thus Place and the NPU were left to make most of the running.

Professor Briggs has shown how the divisions within London radicalism were mirrored in the provinces (**76**). Working-class radicals sought reform firstly as an apocalyptic cure for economic distress, secondly as a consequence of their theory of political rights, and thirdly as a strand in their dream of a new society. By contrast, merchant and manufacturing groups sought increased representation for local interests, whilst remaining fearful of disorder and the 'extreme' aims of Owenites, trade unionists and democrats. The latter seemed to imply the danger of attacks on the capitalist system and property rights.

Birmingham was exceptional in achieving relative class harmony in the reform movement, largely because of the city's small workshops and rapid social mobility, which tended to blur the distinctions between masters and men. There was little labour-saving machinery to throw workers out of jobs, whilst economic fluctuations affected all classes in a similar fashion and promoted class harmony. For these reasons, both the middle and the working classes lined up behind the Birmingham Political Union and endorsed the currency theories of its leader, Thomas Attwood. The influence of the local branch of the National Union of the Working Classes was minimal. In Leicester, middle-class and working-class radicals were able to act together for Reform against their common enemy, the old and corrupt corporation (**82,** ch. 10).

Towns like Manchester and Leeds provided a sharp contrast to Birmingham and Leicester. Manchester's factories opened a wide gulf between masters and men. The result was keen class antagonism and the fragmentation of the local reform movement. Leading industrialists were more anxious about cheap wages, *laissez faire* and public economy than they were about reform. They strongly opposed Birmingham currency theories. The Manchester Political Union, which supported the Reform Bill, was composed mainly of the lower middle-class 'shopocracy' and excluded working men, although it had very little sympathy with the mill owners. It was strongly opposed by a working-class political union, containing many handloom weavers threatened by machinery, which demanded manhood suffrage and the ballot. The 'extreme' views of the latter alienated many of the middle class and prevented them from speaking out as loudly for Reform as their counterparts in Birmingham.

In Leeds there were similar divisions. Here the weavers were also menaced by the power loom and opposed Baines's 'Whig' political union. Some of them formed a universal suffrage political union and spread their message in the *Leeds Patriot*. Others joined the short-time committees of the Factory Movement, led by a Tory squire, Richard Oastler, and a group of Anglican clergy and mill owners opposed to *all* parliamentary reform (**76, 63,** ch. 4, pt. vi). There was a similar pattern in other northern towns, including Bolton and Bradford.

Thus in a number of key provincial centres, industrialisation had produced unbridgeable divisions between the middle- and the working-class reform movements. Moreover, the middle classes themselves were divided in their aims and differed in their degrees of enthusiasm for reform. It may well be that the deep-seated middle-class fear of the threat from below would have inhibited attempts to lead a revolutionary outbreak had the Reform Bill failed, despite the forecasts of Place and the Millite radicals.

The outbreaks of violence that did occur lent little support to the reality of the 'image of revolution'. The London 'Illumination' riots in the spring of 1831 were confined largely to the smashing of unilluminated windows of anti-reformers and were more festive than revolutionary in spirit—a kind of closed shop of celebration. Election riots in Scotland in April consisted of window-smashing and pelting Tories with stones, but such riots were common before 1832 and never, in this case, got out of hand. The London riots of October 1831, following a procession, six thousand strong, to petition the king for reform, resulted in yet more window smashing, as well as assaults on Tory peers. Yet most of the marchers remained orderly and reports of the incidents were inflated as a result of the arrival of news of the Derby and Nottingham disturbances. Cobbett's *Political Register* expressed amazement 'that so little violence should have been committed' (**83,** ch. 4).

Riots at Nottingham and Derby were more serious. Two days of rioting at Nottingham involved the firing of property, including Nottingham Castle (unoccupied and undefended) and a factory. But no lives were lost and order was soon restored when three hundred yeomanry arrived to reinforce the seventy-five troops. The riots were partly the result of the very weak forces of law and order, and partly because of resentment at the Duke of Newcastle, a notorious boroughmonger who victimised reform tenants. In Derby there were three days of rioting. The houses of anti-reformers were burned. A successful attack was mounted on the borough gaol to release prisoners recently arrested. Although troops arrived and quickly restored order, three bystanders had been killed.

Most serious of all were the Bristol riots, which began when Sir Charles Wetherall, Recorder of Bristol and MP for the rotten borough of Boroughbridge, who had just opposed the Reform Bill in Parliament, insisted on visiting the town. For two days, Bristol was in the hands of the rioters. Public buildings, including the bishop's palace, the Mansion House and the custom house, were attacked and razed. Twelve men were killed and over a hundred wounded. Eighty-one prisoners were convicted; four were executed and six given transportation for seven years.

Behind the riots lay intense opposition to the Bristol corporation, hesitancy on the part of the magistrates and inefficiency by the local cavalry commander (later court-martialled). What began as political riots, ended as an orgy of pillage and plunder by unemployed labourers and teenagers; a display which disgusted those of the artisan classes who had initially been involved in the riots. If there had been genuine revolutionary excitement in the country, needing only a spark to set it alight, then surely the ignition would have been provided by the Bristol riots. As it was, order was soon restored. No attempts were made to release the Bristol prisoners, let alone plunge the country into revolution. Rather the reverse; for the Bristol riots frightened the propertied radicals and increased the distance between them and the artisans (**81**). Industrial and agrarian distress, involving rural arson and violent strikes, never became closely linked with the reform movement. Instead it resulted in a revival of the old tradition of primitive economic rioting. In 1832, even in the final crisis, there was a good deal less violence than in the previous year.

Even a weak and disorganised revolutionary impulse has some chance of success if the forces of the established order are impotent. Such an opportunity was available in 1830–2, since public order in the provinces was in the hands of local officials, who lacked professional police forces and were obliged to rely on semitrained yeomanry and untrained special constables (**84**). Troops could be summoned from the Home Office in an emergency, to act as mounted policemen. They were usually able to quell riots without having to fire muskets or use the points of their swords.

While there is no concrete evidence to suggest that the army might have been disloyal in the event of a mass revolutionary outbreak, it is true that there was an overall shortage of troops, who therefore had to be moved quickly from one trouble spot to another. Simultaneous risings in widespread areas of the country would probably have proved too much for the inadequate machinery of public order. The fact that the machinery was never really tested reveals the weakness of the revolutionary threat (**83,** ch. 5).

Though occasionally apprehensive, the government never lost its nerve and shared the panic of local magistrates. Melbourne and his officials at the Home Office were sceptical about the possibility of revolution, although they were willing to take measures against the Rotunda radicals and the working-class political unions. The government's instinct served it correctly, for the threat of revolution in 1830–2 had little reality behind it. Deep economic distress and widespread hatred of the nobility, the Church, boroughmongers and placemen was not the same thing as real revolutionary fervour. One suspects that if politicians had been better informed about the actual state of feeling in the country, and less exposed to the propaganda and wire-pulling of the Benthamite radicals, a 'compromise' Bill might have been the result, instead of the Great Reform Act.

5 The Great Reform Act and Mid-Victorian Politics

THE ACT

The 1832 Reform Act retained the 658 seats of the unreformed system. Fifty-six smaller English boroughs were totally disfranchised. Weymouth lost two of its four members, while thirty other boroughs were deprived of one of their two members. The Act created twenty-two new two-member and twenty one-member boroughs. Seven counties received a third MP and twenty-six two-member counties were divided in half, sending two members for each division. The Isle of Wight was given an MP, while Yorkshire (county) was to elect six members instead of four. Wales obtained three more county members, a new borough (Merthyr Tydfil) and a new district (Swansea). Eight new borough seats were created in Scotland, whilst four large Irish boroughs, plus Dublin University, were given an additional representative.

However, not all the vacancies created, amounting to 126 in England alone, went to new constituencies. The essential conservatism of the Reform Act was underlined by the fact that many 'new' constituencies were merely old ones with enlarged boundaries; whilst many seats went to the counties, thus strengthening the landed interest. The counties now had 253 members, instead of 188; borough representation fell from 465 to 399. Wales, Scotland and Ireland increased their representation, from 169 to 187, compared with that of England, which dropped from 489 to 471. Fourteen of the twenty-two new two-member boroughs were industrial towns, like Manchester, Birmingham, Leeds, Bolton, Oldham and Bradford. But seven two-member seats remained in an already over-represented south. Seats given to London still left it badly under-represented after the Reform Act (**85, 86,** pt. i).

Only the intolerably diseased sections of the old system were completely cut out; many of the constituencies which had their boundaries extended were rotten boroughs which remained in the grip of the landed gentry. There were still enormous variations among the boroughs. Eight had less than two hundred electors; there were still places where fifty voters could return an MP. Thirty-five boroughs had less than three hundred electors: Liverpool had 11,300. Of course, electorates increased as wealth and population grew, especially after 1843. Certainly the boroughs had a disproportionately stronger voice in the House of Commons than the counties. Boroughs had 43 per cent of the electorate and 62 per cent of the seats, whereas counties had 57 per cent of the electorate and only 38 per cent of the seats. But it must be remembered that many of the small boroughs were rural in nature and therefore reinforced the landed interest.

Important anomalies remained. Despite the fact that many southern rotten boroughs had gone, the overrepresentation of southern England was almost as striking a feature of the new electoral system as the old. Ten southern counties, with a population of 3,300,000, had 156 seats. The urban areas of Middlesex, Lancashire and the West Riding had 3,700,000 people, but only 58 MPs. Scotland had three times the population of Wales, but less than twice as many seats. Ireland had three times the population of Scotland, but less than double the representation. The Irish Reform Act intensified, rather than reduced, the influence of landlords and priests; while the Scots Reform Act, drafted with blithe disregard for Scottish feudal law, introduced as many anomalies and inconsistencies as it removed (**92**).

In the English counties, the 40*s* freehold franchise was retained, but votes were also given to £10 copyholders, £10 long leaseholders, £50 medium leaseholders and £50 tenants. There was a new uniform franchise in the boroughs: occupiers, as owners or tenants, of buildings of an annual value of £10, provided that such occupiers had twelve months residence and had paid their rates and taxes. Voting was still open. Most of those who held the pre-1832 franchises were permitted to continue voting in their lifetime. Plural voting was permitted, but paupers (in boroughs), peers, customs officials, excise men, revenue officers, post office men, policemen, magistrates, aliens, lunatics, minors and women were disqualified from voting. Elaborate registration procedure kept off the electoral rolls many of those otherwise qualified (**100**). The unreformed electorate had been about 478,000; it now rose to 813,000 out of a UK population of 24 million. In other words, the electorate was one-thirtieth of the population, or, more realistically, one in seven of every adult male in the United Kingdom (one in five in England, one in eight in Scotland and one in twenty in Ireland).

The relation of the new franchises to class structure is difficult to assess, partly because of considerable regional variations, partly because of the difficulty of defining classes in this period. Still, there is little doubt that ordinary agricultural labourers in the counties were completely excluded. In the boroughs, the £10 householder varied in social status according to the prevailing level of house values. In London and Manchester, for example, the £10 qualification included a number of skilled working men. On the whole, however, the new borough voters were *petit bourgeois* or middle-class. It is likely that fewer working men possessed the vote after 1832 than before. In 1830 working men had been a majority of electorates in constituencies which returned 130 members. Most lost their votes in 1832 (**86**, ch. 4; **82**, ch. 10, **97, 95**).

THE SYSTEM

The reformed electoral system, which has been so brilliantly described by Professor Gash, was a mixture of old and new. The social composition of the House of Commons changed only very slowly. Parliament still mainly consisted of aristocrats and country gentlemen (**101**). It has been calculated that the Parliament of 1841 had 342 sons of peers, baronets, or near relations of peers, plus a further 240 who are classified as 'landed gentry' (**102, 103**). Together they formed 71 per cent of the House of Commons. No more than 22 per cent was actively engaged in the operation or control of a business. As late as 1865, the landed interest still accounted for 44 per cent of members. This situation was partly a result of the tendency, apparent even in industrial constituencies, to elect 'gentlemen' and social superiors (**97**). Even militant Dissenters were frequently content to be represented by Anglican Whigs.

Probably another reason for the slow change in the social composition of Parliament was the fact that members needed a large private income (**89**, chs. 1, 2). Macaulay had to leave the Commons and find a job, while Disraeli survived only by obscure financial transactions, which included marriage (**147**, ch. 7). Until 1858 county members had to possess a £600 landed estate; borough members a £300 one. In fact these qualifications could easily be evaded. More to the point were high election expenses. Official expenses were substantial: as high as between £600 and £1000 for counties and £400 for boroughs.

Unofficial expenses could be even higher. Besides the inevitable bills for canvassing, polling booths and hired gangs of supporters, there remained the traditional expenditure on food, drink and 'entertainment'. There was no effective statutory restriction on election expenses before 1883 (**172,** ch. 1). A contested election brought money into the constituency; candidates were all too often regarded as little more than milch cows. Even the new voters expected some kind of bribe, however disguised. At the 1841 election, individual votes were sold brazenly for £4 at Penryn, £7 at Sudbury and £15 at Ipswich. The Nottingham election cost the successful candidates £12,000 and the unsuccessful ones £17,000. Even an uncontested election for a pocket borough could cost between £200 and £400. If there were a petition to unseat the successful candidate after a contested election, then heavy legal expenses were involved (**86,** chs. 5, 6, 7).

A successful candidate at Wallingford in 1852 voiced a common complaint when he declared that he had had to contend with 'bribery, intimidation, and every species of undue influence'. In a system where influence counted for more than opinion, the methods of exerting it varied (**86,** ch. 8). Relatively peaceful methods involved eviction from tenancies, dismissal from employment and withdrawal of custom from shops and firms. More forcible methods included 'cooping': holding electors, usually in a state of inebriation, prisoner until the poll was over. This was a common practice at Leicester and Nottingham (**99**). At their worst, elections could involve bloody clashes between rival gangs of hired thugs, the beating up of rival supporters, or even death. In the carnival atmosphere of nomination day, candidates on the hustings were pelted with everything from rotten vegetables and horse dung to stones and human refuse. In the absence of police forces, elections often became so violent that the military had to be summoned. Sometimes they opened fire, as at Wolverhampton in 1835.

Violence at elections was taken remarkably lightly until late in the Victorian age. The prudish and the genteel, less common before 1850 than after, feared election time with considerable justification. Professor Gash has pointed out how Dickens's description of the

Eatanswill election in *Pickwick Papers* was 'a pale and euphemistic version of the contemporary scene'. Radicals were no more ready to eschew violence and intimidation than were the traditional gentry. Neither were the labouring classes. Excluded from the electorate in most constituencies before the prosperous mid-Victorian years, they still played a significant role at elections. Non-electors held meetings, questioned candidates, formed the mobs and wielded the powerful weapon of boycotting and exclusive dealing on retailers and craftsmen. In a sense, non-electors voted when out shopping (**128**, ch. 2).

Some parts of the most diseased sections of the unreformed system survived 1832. The ancient trade of boroughmonger still existed, for it remained possible to purchase a seat in the House of Commons. Constituencies where the election depended almost solely on a cash transaction included Stafford, Lewes, Ipswich, Sudbury and St Albans. The two latter were disfranchised in 1841 for gross corruption. At Stafford in 1832, one election agent spent over £1000 in bribes on 400–500 electors. Bribery and treating were never more prevalent than in the decades after the 1832 Reform Act (**172**, ch. 1). Bribery was the crucial factor determining the result.in many elections; candidates avoided it at their peril. Legislation to curb it remained largely ineffective until after the 1867 Reform Act [**doc. 26**].

Much influence, now regarded as corrupt, was recognised as legitimate by contemporary opinion. It included the influence of masters over employees, landlords over tenants and clergymen over their congregations (**86**, ch. 8, **88**, introduction). It was as much a sense of gratitude and obligation as fear of sanctions which made it a rarity for tenants to defy their landlords. Poll books issued after elections reveal that, in the counties, groups of villages and parishes tended to follow their landlords in block votes (**93**). The House of Lords still retained some influence over the commons, *via* the younger sons, friends and supporters of peers. Family boroughs still flourished, perhaps the most famous being Tamworth, which returned Peel. Although the days of the great eighteenth-century borough proprietors, owning five or six boroughs, had gone, patrons still had power. Gash reckons that after 1832 about fifty boroughs with seventy members, in England and Wales alone, depended on the influence of peers and landlords. Such boroughs usually returned members of the proprietor's family, but they also came in handy for ministers defeated in other constituencies and for the return of bright young men. The young Gladstone, for example, was elected at the Duke of Newcastle's rotten borough of Newark in 1832 (**98**). In many of the medium and small boroughs, rural in nature, the dominant landlord was able to tighten his grip by the wholesale creation of £10 houses.

The complex operation of various kinds of influence proved an obstacle to the free and clear expression of the political views of the electorate on national issues. Of course in many constituencies politics were local rather than national, and 'national issues' meant very little. Hence the emergence of popular constituency parties was a slow process. The large number of small electorates meant that there were few such popular associations before 1860. Also important in this context was the vast number of compromises, where agreement was reached between the various 'interests' in a constituency, in order to avoid the turmoil and expense of an election. Between 1832 and 1847 less than half the total seats were contested at any single election.

Nevertheless, parties were stronger between 1835 and 1846 than they had been earlier, although there was not the strong party discipline which acts as the lubricating oil of the engine of government in the modern constitution. Party became more important to governments than patronage. Both royal and government boroughs survived 1832, but became less useful for ensuring majorities (**86,** chs. 12–14). In 1835 and again in 1841, parties proved sufficiently strong to impose prime ministers on the monarch. This was a new trend, unusual under the unreformed system, although its impact was softened by the break up of the Tory party in 1846 (**87**). The importance of the registration clauses of the 1832 Act led to the establishment of local political associations and registration committees, whose primary task was to get voters on or off the register (**100, 97**) [**doc. 12**]. However, connections between the local associations and the parties at the centre were usually tenuous. To some extent the gap was filled by political clubs (**86,** ch. 15). The Tory Carlton Club was founded in 1832 and the Whig Reform Club in 1836. Under the guidance of Peel, the assiduous Tory election agent, F. R. Bonham, organised a remarkable revival of the shattered Tory party in the 1830s, a revival based on the Carlton Club. In 1841 the party returned to office with a substantial majority.

NADIR OF REFORM

The strengthening of the party system and the decline of government electoral patronage were both results of the 1832 Reform Act. On the other hand, a major blow against 'modern' developments was struck by the manner in which Peel repealed the Corn Laws in 1846. Historians have been preoccupied with the social and economic effects of repeal, now seen to have been exaggerated (**110, 112**). But the political effects were of great importance. By rejecting the advice of Cobden and refusing to go to the country on the repeal issue, Peel dismissed the notion that the people had a right to choose a government, as opposed to a House of Commons. Policy must be decided by the government, not by the electorate, otherwise it would be democracy with a vengeance. Peel was careful to avoid democracy in this sense by accepting gradual, instead of immediate, repeal, thus averting a clash with the House of Lords and a constitutional crisis akin to that of 1832. For there was no knowing what might be the result of such a crisis in what was the age of the Chartists as well as that of the Anti-Corn Law League. Thus Peel preserved the political supremacy of the landed classes and made sure that there was no major advance along the road to democracy in 1846, even if it meant losing office, splitting the Tory party and earning, paradoxically, the hatred of large sections of the landed interest (**111**).

After 1846 the chances of further reform seemed slim. Chartism had alienated the middle classes and made a class alliance for Reform impossible [**doc. 13**]. Joseph Sturge's Complete Suffrage Union proved a failure (**106**, ch. 11). Chartism itself lost impetus after 1842. Cobden and Bright attempted to shift the energy and organisation of the repeal agitation into a movement for parliamentary reform, although Cobden was less hopeful than his partner [**doc. 15**]. Yet the coalition which had supported the Anti-Corn Law League quickly fell apart after repeal, whilst Bright and Cobden became unpopular when they opposed the Crimean War (**113, 133,** ch. 3). Their attempts to launch a new reform movement never attracted mass support. Class antagonisms diminished in what has been termed 'the age of equipoise' (**114**). Mild inflation gave an illusion of economic prosperity and took the edge off demands for parliamentary reform (**192**, ch. 9).

The middle classes were too varied, too limited in education, experience, breadth of outlook and amount of leisure to pose a viable alternative to aristocratic government. They were a social force rather than a political force and most of them recognised the fact (**128,** introduction). The Crimean War tended to promote class unity, for the inadequacies of aristocratic government, revealed in its scandalous prosecution of the war, had a delayed impact. Meanwhile liberal movements abroad, in Italy, Poland and Hungary, tended to divert attention from the domestic front. A succession of Palmerstonian administrations was a sign of the stability of the political system at a time when radicalism was fragmented and party labels had little meaning (**116**) [**doc. 15, 16**].

This is not to deny that, beneath the surface, there were changes favourable to another parliamentary reform campaign. Religious revivals and the growth of a provincial cheap daily press helped to spread popular Liberalism in the 1850s and 1860s (**128,** ch. 2). Thousands of skilled artisans were motivated by the gospel of individual self-improvement to join the new Liberal associations. Labouring men were much less keen to seek separate political expression than they had been in the age of the Chartists. Even in 1842 men like William Lovett, Henry Vincent and Robert Lowery had seen the need for close relationships between the middle and working classes if Reform were to be achieved (**109**). Such close relations became the pattern in the 1850s and 1860s, affecting even 'Socialists' like Ernest Jones (**131**). Hence the Liberal party at constituency level began to be radicalised. The fact that national politics seemed stagnant was partly a result of the gap which opened up between the parliamentary and the constituency Liberal parties.

6 Whigs and Liberals

REFORMERS

Reformers in the 1860s were on solid ground when they argued that the electoral system was still grossly unrepresentative. Despite the continued expansion of commercial and industrial Britain since 1832, Parliament in the 1860s was still fundamentally aristocratic. After the 1865 election, there sat in the House of Commons 116 sons of peers and their relations, 109 baronets and their relations, plus about a hundred commoners related to the peerage. This aristocratic element, evenly divided between the Conservatives and Liberals, amounted to about half the House of Commons. Cabinets were still composed almost exclusively of members of traditional ruling families; Gladstone and Disraeli were dazzling exceptions. Such a monopoly of power by the old ruling class, the landed interest in politics, was partly a result of the force of tradition and deference and partly the result of the restricted electorate. Most of all, however, it was a reflection of the maldistribution of seats.

The south and west remained strongly overrepresented in the system, a situation which was aggravated as such areas as East Anglia and south-west England continued to decline as the North and Midlands expanded. In 1865 one-fifth of the electorate of England and Wales returned 328 MPs—half the House of Commons. The nine largest boroughs, with a combined population of over three millions, sent only eighteen MPs to Westminster. Eleven small boroughs, with a total population of only 44,000, sent seventeen members. Bradford had a population of 106,000 in 1861, but an electorate of only 4000. Leeds had 7000 voters out of 200,000 inhabitants in 1865. Out of a UK population of 30 million in 1865, the total electorate was 1,430,000.

In rural communities—the counties and the smaller boroughs— the landed interest was still firmly in control, especially since many of the small towns were virtual pocket boroughs. The impact of middle-class votes on the electoral system tended to be softened by the unequal distribution of seats, which concentrated the middle-class franchise in a few urban constituencies. The same was largely true of working-class votes, calculated in 1866 to account for 26 per cent of the whole (**144,** ch. 2).

Even some of the party leaders found the system unsatisfactory. Russell had regarded the 1832 Reform Act as 'final' (hence his nickname 'Finality Jack'), but abandoned this position in 1851. In the 1860s, both he and Gladstone became convinced that efficient government needed the stimulus of a wider electorate; although neither was interested in manhood suffrage, which they felt would imply a real transfer of power to the working class. Gladstone was especially impressed by the 'respectable' elite among the artisan classes. Pro-reform arguments of 1832 were resurrected: that the continued exclusion of a powerful social group from the franchise might invite serious assaults on the institutions of the country. This time, the 'labour aristocracy' of skilled and responsible workers was the powerful group. Gladstone saw politics as primarily a moral exercise. Rational reform would act as a stimulus to moral improvement. Working men of the 'respectable' classes deserved votes as a reward for good behaviour.

There was considerable evidence for such arguments. The expansion of industries like building, iron, engineering, shipbuilding and railways, meant the rapid growth of numbers of skilled men. Such men formed the bulk of the 'labour aristocracy', divided from the unskilled by their higher incomes, superior housing, membership of churches, chapels, the cooperative movement and friendly societies. Many of them sent their children to school, read the penny press, invested in savings banks and generally adopted a way of life akin to that of the lower middle classes. Middle-class attitudes of thrift, self-reliance, sexual 'prudence' and self-improvement further divided the new working class elite from the mass of the unskilled (**117–122**) [**doc. 14**].

Gladstone was especially impressed by what he termed 'the self-command, self-control, respect for order, patience under suffering, confidence in the law, regard for superiors' exhibited by the Lancashire mechanics at the time of the cotton famine during the American Civil War. Reformers argued that such men could safely be given the franchise, since their acceptance of middle-class attitudes would cause them to defer to social superiors and to eschew 'socialist' ideas. Not even John Bright wished to enfranchise the residuum of unskilled labourers; those regarded by the propertied classes as irresponsible, corrupt, immoral and liable to support extremist attacks on the sacred rights of property and the divine laws of the free market.

Middle-class reformers in the provinces looked to a further extension of the franchise as a means of breaking the aristocratic monopoly of political power; something which the 1832 Reform Act and Corn Law repeal in 1846 had conspicuously failed to do. This would enable them to further their own aims, many of which were bound up with the programme of militant Dissent (**128,** ch. 2). Whig cabinets, the established church, the game laws, 'aristocratic' foreign policy, an unreformed army and civil service, the exclusion of Dissenters from the universities: all were important targets for the reformers. To get rid of such 'abuses' would require the creation of a more popular Liberal party than existed under the Palmerstonian regimes of the 1850s and early 1860s.

An enfranchised working-class elite would serve as crucial reinforcements for a campaign to push the Palmerstonian Whig-Liberal coalition in a radical direction. The basic strategy of such a campaign would be to attack the privileged position of the landed classes in British society. Moreover, to enfranchise a select group of 're-spectable' and deferent working men would be to bind them still further to the middle classes, thus helping to consolidate class harmony. Without the status symbol of the franchise, the labour aristocracy might be tempted to act as the spearhead of an attack on the capitalist system, an attack based on increased trade union activity and strikes. Many reformers were also employers and tended often to regard parliamentary reform as a means of avoiding a powerful anti-capitalist movement. This inclined them to seek only a 'safe' measure of reform. They had no wish to encourage manhood suffrage, or to subscribe to theories which held that working men should possess the franchise as a natural right. The suffrage must be the reward only of those who accepted middle-class nostrums, including self-help, independence, property rights, individualism and *laissez-faire* economics (**28**).

ANTI-REFORMERS

Lowe and Cranborne were the leading spokesmen for the anti-reformers (**27, 30**) [**doc. 20, 23a**]. They saw the working classes as corrupt, brutal and ignorant. To give them political power would lead to attacks on property, individual freedom and the free market. Disinterested and efficient government would become impossible. Working men would employ their votes for merely selfish motives: to drain wealth away from the upper classes to themselves and, by indiscriminate attacks on 'privilege', tear at the fabric of the social structure.

At the level of practical politics, the Liberals were the party of reform. Yet they were more afraid of enfranchising the residuum than were the Tories. Their formula for reform was a restricted one, a £5 or £6 borough franchise; certainly not household suffrage. Bright, the leader of provincial radicalism, was perfectly satisfied with the Reform Bill of 1866. Gladstone spoke of household suffrage as 'beyond the wants and wishes of the time' and argued that a £5 rating franchise was the most that could safely be granted. These limited Liberal proposals were based on their belief that the labour aristocracy would vote Liberal; while the residuum, deferent and stupid, would vote Tory. The Conservative party saw that such proposals were partly designed to increase the number of Liberal votes and hence opposed them. On the other hand, they had less reason to fear household suffrage. They believed, with some justification, that the classes at the bottom of the social ladder were conservative in politics as well as in temperament [**docs. 22, 25**]. The eight boroughs in 1866. with a working class majority in their electorate returned five Liberals and nine Conservatives (**150**).

Liberal theory easily lent itself to sustaining the case against reform. Liberals lacked the Conservative belief in a natural and deferential social order. On the contrary, they saw society as a mass of individuals, independent of each other and pursuing their own private interests at the expense of those of other people. Politics was one method of imposing order on society; changes in the political system, even small ones, could therefore jeopardise the social structure. This helps to explain why Liberals worried rather more than Conservatives about the details of reform. Tories believed that the forces of deference and tradition would preserve the social structure despite major political changes.

Robert Lowe was a Liberal intellectual in politics, who used pure Utilitarian arguments against reform with devastating logic. He depicted the individual as independent, isolated and self-seeking. To grant anything approaching democracy would be to remove necessary restraints on naturally selfish behaviour and to knock the props from civilised social and political relations (**27, 30**) [**doc. 20**]. Many liberal intellectuals became more anxious about the implications of democracy as it seemed to become a political possibility. The liberal concept of the 'active' citizen, one who would increase his moral virtue by participation in politics, owed a great deal to John Stuart Mill's *Representative Government* (1861). Yet even Mill refused to allow that the unpropertied masses were 'responsible' enough to become active citizens. Power must still be in the hands of an elite (**24**). A popular democratic parliament was unfitted to conduct the skilled administration of a modern state. Democracy might lead to mere mediocrity and the rejection of the views and influence of the 'leading spirits . . . the first minds in the country', those who were motivated by reason rather than self-interest [**doc. 18**].

Matthew Arnold mounted a scathing attack on semi-educated middle-class 'Philistines' in *Culture and Anarchy* (1869). In 1873 James Fitzjames Stephen published *Liberty, Equality, Fraternity*, a withering assault on the liberal tradition and on Utilitarian belief in rational progress. Stephen wrote of 'a tyrannical democracy which will change the whole face of society and destroy all that I love or respect in our institutions'. Many Liberal intellectuals were confirmed in the cowardice of their convictions by Lowe's arguments. In a speech delivered in 1865, he declared:

> Because I am a Liberal and know that by pure and clear intelligence alone can the cause of progress be promoted, I regard as one of the greatest dangers with which this country can be threatened a proposal to subvert the existing order of things, and to transfer power from the hands of property and intelligence to the hands of men whose daily life is necessarily employed in daily struggle for existence.

OVERTURE TO THE SECOND REFORM ACT

The panic among intellectuals began in the mid-1860s, when reform began to be practical politics (**137**). Before 1865 the chances of reform seemed slim indeed. Chartism was virtually dead as a potent political force. With its passing, the working-class political movement became fragmented. Among the fissiparous tendencies were the growing differential between skilled and unskilled, the lack of a political philosophy which gave working men a clear and independent political function, and the seduction of working men by middle-class movements and institutions. The working classes exhibited a kind of split-consciousness. In the economic sphere there was a good deal of militant trade unionism and an unwillingness to accept middle-class economic shibboleths; in politics, however, the Chartist legacy was soon spent (**129,** ch. 7). The result was that, according to Bagehot, 'the mass of the people yield obedience to a select few' [**doc. 21**].

Mention has been made earlier of the long period of relative political stalemate at Westminster which succeeded the repeal of the Corn Laws. The majority of MPs were Anglicans and landowners, who cared little for social reform and even less for parliamentary reform. Indeed, there was an agreement between Palmerston and Derby in the 1860s to avoid the reform question. There had been a number of Reform Bills introduced in the House of Commons earlier, although they gained little support other than that of the seventy or so Radicals on the fringe of the Palmerstonian coalition. These were the heirs of the Anti-Corn Law League; Bright and Cobden were still their leaders. One section of the radicals was composed of manufacturers, commercial men and journalists; the other comprised a small group of radical country gentlemen.

However, these 'advanced Liberals' could make little impression on their colleagues in the House of Commons. Locke King introduced motions for giving votes to £10 occupiers in the counties, Edward Baines those for a £6 borough franchise. Neither had any success. In 1851 Russell drafted a Bill which would reduce the county tenant franchise to £20 and the borough qualification to £10 rateable value, with a complex scheme of indirect voting. It was rejected by the Cabinet. In 1852 Russell introduced a Bill in the Commons, with the same franchise provisions as that of the previous year, plus the grouping of sixty-seven small boroughs with neighbouring unrepresented towns. Radicals opposed the Bill because it did not go far enough; Whigs and Tories denounced it as going too far. Russell was obliged to withdraw it.

He tried again with another Bill in 1854. The county franchise was to be given to £10 occupiers; the borough qualification was to be £6 rateable value. To calm the fears of those who dreaded a flood of new electors, special 'fancy franchises' were to be given to certain groups: £2 direct taxpayers, university graduates, those with a salary of £100 a year, those with an annual income of £10 from government stock, or those with £50 in a savings bank. Once more the Bill was withdrawn, partly because Palmerston disapproved, partly because of Radical opposition to such a mild measure, and also because of the outbreak of the Crimean War. There were only eighteen petitions in favour of the Bill from the whole country (**130**, ch. 2).

In 1858 the initiative on reform was seized by Disraeli, who suggested to Derby that the question might do something to revive the sagging fortunes of a Tory party apparently doomed to exclusion from genuine political power. Disraeli pointed out that there was no logical reason why the Whigs should have a monopoly of the reform question. He also pointed out that in 1832 they had passed an Act which served their own electoral interests. Privately, Disraeli was in favour of a drastic measure. He was already convinced that many working men would support the monarchy, the empire and the Conservative party. A limited measure would only confirm the Whig monopoly of office. But Disraeli could not persuade the Cabinet to accept these views and the Bill, when it appeared in 1858, was a very conservative one (**147**, ch. 18).

The county occupancy franchise was lowered to £10, that in the boroughs remained unaltered, except that borough freehold voters were to cast their votes in boroughs, not counties. This last clause was designed, of course, to strengthen the landed interest. As in Russell's 1854 Bill, there was a batch of 'fancy franchises' (the phrase is Bright's). There was to be little redistribution. Once again, the Bill pleased nobody. Radicals regarded it as a product of mere political expediency, as indeed it was. The gentry felt it to be superfluous. When Russell's motion against the Bill was carried, Derby and Disraeli resigned.

At the time of its formation in 1859, the Palmerston-Russell ministry was dependent on Radical votes. In any case, Palmerston had decided two years earlier that the Whigs ought to try to do something on the Reform question (**141**). Consequently Russell introduced a Bill in 1860. It proposed a £6 rental qualification in the boroughs and a £10 franchise in the counties. Radicals again found it too mild, whilst many Whigs regarded it as simply unnecessary. Tories opposed it on the grounds that it threatened the landed interest. Debate on the merits and demerits of the Bill petered out and Russell let it die, unmourned. There were no further Reform Bills until that of 1866. Other matters, especially questions of foreign policy, diverted the attention of the ministry from the question. The party truce against reform was resurrected, and operated until Palmerston's death in 1865.

When his Bill of 1860 failed, Russell complained: 'The apathy of the country is undeniable. Nor is it a transient humour, it seems rather a confirmed habit of mind.' The hostility of Parliament to reform would be overcome only by 'a great tide of public opinion' and there was no sign of it. In 1859 Bright attempted to stir up an agitation in support of a £6 borough rental franchise, but the campaign proved a damp squib. Enthusiasm in towns like Birmingham, Manchester and Bradford was not echoed elsewhere in the country. Disillusioned, Bright abandoned the question until 1865 (**136, 133,** pt. iii, **134,** ch. 8).

By 1863, however, there were signs of a revival. The stimulus came from abroad. The Italian question in 1859–60 had tended to reconcile working men with the Palmerston government and turn them against Bright. The American Civil War had the opposite effect. It was seen by many as the testing time of democracy in the West. If the 'Great Experiment' survived, then democracy was proved to be both stable and efficient. It may be that the American question only confirmed Englishmen in their existing prejudices (**150**), but meetings held throughout industrial England in support of the Northern cause created an atmosphere of enthusiasm for democracy and antagonism towards the landed gentry (many of whom supported the South) that could easily be switched into a reform campaign (**124–127, 133,** pt. ii, sec. xii).

The next stimulus to 'a great tide of public opinion' came from an unexpected quarter. In a debate in 1864 on the reduction of the borough franchise, Gladstone produced his celebrated sentence: 'I venture to say that every man who is not presumably incapacitated by some consideration of personal unfitness or of political danger is morally entitled to come within the pale of the constitution [provided that this does not lead to] sudden or violent or excessive, or intoxicating change.' His qualifications in the sentence were ignored. Radicals saw Gladstone as an overnight convert to extension of the franchise, basing his belief on a doctrine of moral right. In truth, Gladstone was much less of a democrat than those who rallied to his name imagined. His Canningite Tory origins marked him for life.

His religious beliefs, his faith in the political role of the landed aristocracy and his desire to maintain class harmony, all prevented him from becoming the unambiguous champion of urban Dissenters, businessmen and the working classes. But few members of the public proved able or willing to perceive the ambiguities in Gladstone's richly complex character. Almost in spite of himself he became a popular hero, delivering speeches in the provinces. He seemed to many a much more satisfactory reform leader than Bright, who lacked education, breadth of outlook and a secure position at the centre of political power.

It appeared that an expanding and changing popular Liberal party would soon impel Gladstone to try to pass a comprehensive Reform Bill. Not only was there the influence of the nonconformist revival, the growing provincial press, popular constituency organisations and the forces of organised labour, but there was also a new element—the reform pressure groups which began to agitate on the question.

In April 1864 the National Reform Union was founded. It was essentially an association of Lancashire merchants and manufacturers, meeting in the old Manchester headquarters of the Anti-Corn Law League. Branches were established throughout the country, especially in the industrial areas, attracting Nonconformist clergymen and progressive Liberal politicians, as well as businessmen. It aimed to demonstrate that the middle and working classes shared common political aims and could work together in relative harmony. Implicit in this aim was an attempt to choke at birth any separatist working class political movement (**118,** chs. 1, 3). The programme of the National Reform Union included triennial parliaments, the ballot, equal distribution of seats and a ratepayer franchise. It studiously avoided the phrase 'manhood suffrage' in order not to offend the middle classes.

The Reform League was also founded in 1864, as a byproduct of English enthusiasm for Italian liberty (**123**). It originated in a committee established to welcome Garibaldi to London, although the subsequent meeting was broken up by the police. Its programme was more radical than that of the Reform Union, for the League was committed to manhood suffrage as well as the ballot. While the League lacked the wealth of the Union, it had the advantage of numbers. It succeeded in attracting large numbers of working men, including trade unionists, former Chartists and members of the newly formed First International. The London Trades Council and George Potter's London Working Men's Association were also associated with the Reform League.

Both the League and the Union looked to Bright and Gladstone as parliamentary leaders who would overthrow the dominance of the Whigs in the Liberal party by means of parliamentary reform. Relations between the two reform organisations varied in time and place. In Manchester, for example, there was little love lost (**131**), but in Bradford they cooperated closely and appeared at each other's meetings. Relations certainly became very close when the reform crisis began in 1866 and both agreed to sink their differences in a common campaign for the Reform Bill. The financial role of the National Reform Union should not be underestimated; wealthy industrialist members gave a great deal of money to the Reform League, without which the latter would have found it very difficult to survive (**130,** ch. 6; **129,** ch. 9).

Yet differences between the two bodies could not be completely papered over. The Union was essentially a body within the Liberal party, bent on minimising the influence of Whig elements in the party and increasing that of the industrial middle classes. The latter would then be capable of more successful attacks on privilege in the Church, education, the tax system, the army and the civil service.

The Reform League was not so closely connected with the Liberal party. Its trade union members in particular saw parliamentary reform as an essential preliminary to assaults on the industrial front, assaults which would be most unwelcome to the employers who formed the hard core of the Reform Union. Some Positivist intellectual members of the League even sought to create an independent working-class movement (**118,** ch. 6). However, at the time of the reform crisis of 1866–7, the differences were glossed over in a common agitation for reform and against the aristocracy, with Bright standing at the head of the movement.

THE REFORM BILL OF 1866

Reform was not much of an issue at the 1865 elections; candidates tended to mention it as something of an afterthought. None spoke in favour of manhood suffrage. It was still the golden age of independent members, with no strict party discipline or election programme. The Liberals were returned with a majority of about seventy. Then, on 18 October, Palmerston died. His death ended the party truce against reform and raised the spirits of the radical wing of the Liberal party, which now looked to Gladstone to provide leadership in pushing the party in a leftward direction. Palmerston's death raised obvious dangers for the Conservatives. For a number of years they had been in relative decline. They were still based solidly on the landed interest, at a time when the social and economic importance of the land was beginning to fade. In the early 1860s, those with conservative instincts had looked to Palmerston rather than to Derby. This pattern was broken by Palmerston's death. If Russell and Gladstone succeeded in passing a measure of reform tailored to their own electoral advantage, where only 'safe' Liberal voters would be enfranchised, then the Conservative party would be doomed. Hence the Tory leaders were careful never to oppose reform in principle; only Liberal versions of it. Disraeli's strategy had two main elements, both designed to sustain the fortunes of the party. The first was to pose as the party of property and safety, thus attracting those who panicked at the sight of Radical democracy. The second was to be ready with some plan of reform, in case the political situation demanded that the Conservatives grasp the reform nettle. Either way, the important thing for Tory leaders was to make sure that Gladstone did not pass a measure which benefited only the Liberal party (**157**, introduction).

Russell succeeded Palmerston as Prime Minister, with Gladstone Chancellor of the Exchequer. Both men were glad to be out of Palmerston's shadow and 'unmuzzled' at last. But Russell realised the need to keep the party together and did all he could to woo the Conservative wing. When this tactic failed and most leading Palmerstonians refused to join the ministry, Russell was obliged to turn to the radicals. James Stansfield and W. E. Forster were invited to join the administration.

It was Forster who pitchforked Russell into introducing a Reform Bill. Russell had hoped to postpone the question for at least two years, by appointing a Commission of Inquiry into the electoral system. He realised that, although the Liberal backbenchers were willing to support a reforming programme of social, Church and economic issues, they were likely to resist the thought of abdicating power to an organised urban working-class movement. Yet Forster insisted on making a speech at Bradford on 22 November, where he declared: 'The country not only demands reform, but it expects it, and the government are aware that it is necessary to their existence, to their continuance as a government, that they should meet this demand.' Russell needed Radical support; so he took Forster into the ministry, abandoned the idea of a Commission and planned the introduction of a Reform Bill. Drafting the Bill was no easy matter, because of regional variations in the electoral pattern and the lack of reliable statistics. There were infinite variations in both house values and methods of paying rates. Russell himself was willing to go only so far as enfranchising borough owners and tenants of houses with a clear annual value of £6, although such people were difficult to define on the statute book (**144,** ch. 4).

By this time Russell was becoming tired and not a little confused. He subsequently lost his grip on affairs. Details were left to Gladstone. Palmerstonian elements in the Cabinet (Clarendon, Grey, Somerset, Cardwell and Stanley) wanted a postponement of reform, especially when the Poor Law returns revealed that a substantial number of working men already possessed the franchise on the 1832 £10 qualification. They also showed that there was an uncomfortably large amount of urban housing valued between £6 and £10. Nevertheless, bombarded with encouraging messages from Bright, Russell and Gladstone stood firm, although they avoided a redistribution scheme for the time being, for fear of antagonising the right wing of the party.

They aimed to add a substantial proportion of the working class to the electorate, but without threatening the supremacy of the ruling classes. Realisation of this aim was not easy. Information on levels of rents and rates was so contradictory, or even lacking in some cases, that the details of the Bill led to bitter arguments between various sections of the Liberal party. These wrangles continued until less than a week before the Bill was due to be introduced in the Commons. Finally, and somewhat in haste, a £7 annual gross rental was chosen for the borough franchise (**144,** ch. 4).

The Bill of 1866 was in fact less extensive than that of Russell in 1860. A £7 rental qualification would enfranchise about 156,000, of whom about 144,000 were judged to be working men. According to Gladstone, such men would earn at least 26s a week; hence the Bill would exclude the unskilled labourers of Bright's 'residuum'.The vote was also to be given to £10 lodgers in boroughs and £50 savings bank depositors in counties. The county occupation franchise was to be dropped from £50 to £14, which would add 172,000 middle-class voters, assumed to be Liberals, to the county electorate. County votes were given to borough Liberals by allowing county leaseholders and copyholders resident in boroughs to vote in the county where their holdings were situated. In all, the 1866 Bill would have enfranchised 400,000 men, about half of them working-class. The conservatism of the Bill is underlined when it is realised that the existing borough electorate of 36 per cent of total male occupiers would be raised to a mere 51 per cent. In England and Wales, one man in every four would have a vote, instead of one man in five (**144,** ch. 4; **145,** ch. 2).

Radicals were disappointed that the Bill failed to concede household suffrage and the ballot. Whigs regarded the £7 rental franchise as not a sufficiently selective instrument to limit extension to the 'safe' labour aristocracy. At first the Conservatives acted cautiously. Derby seemed reluctant to attack the Bill with vigour, while Disraeli moved very carefully. His own position in the Tory party was far from secure. He cared little about the level of the borough franchise, being more concerned to defend the position of the landed interest. What soon became clear to him was that he was being presented with a unique opportunity of smashing the Liberal party. Here was a chance to prise apart the Whigs and Radicals, which would bring about the fall of the government and the return of the Conservatives to office, perhaps led by himself (**145,** ch. 2; **147,** ch. 20).

It was too good an opening to miss and Disraeli was not the man to miss it. He avoided an open attack, preferring to push Palmerstonian anti-reformers into leading the opposition to the Bill, with Tories lending flank support. An understanding was reached, whereby Disraeli and Cranborne pledged Conservative support for Elcho and Lowe when they attacked their own government's Bill from the Liberal backbenches.

Robert Lowe was the main anti-reform speaker in the debates on the 1866 Bill. Arguing brilliantly from high intellectual principles, he warned that the measure would lead to the destruction of the social hierarchy and the confiscation of property. Democracy would inevitably bring vulgar demagogues to power and result in government as inefficient as it was selfish. France, Australia and America were depicted as examples of the evils of democratic government. According to Lowe, members of the traditional ruling class were civilised, well educated and disinterested. Working men, by contrast, were crude, brutal and lacking in moral worth [**doc. 20**]. In a series of splendid debates, Lowe was answered by Bright [**doc. 19**], who stressed the progress working men had made in wealth, manners and education (**27, 30, 132**).

Bright cut little ice with the landed magnates who, led by Elcho, formed the 'Cave of Adullam' to resist the Reform Bill. Members of the 'Cave' feared the enfranchisement of working men as a blow to the political supremacy of the landed interest; neither did they relish the prospect of higher election expenses which would follow an enlarged electorate. They were also motivated by fear of Gladstone. They disliked his dictatorial parliamentary manner, his Anglo-Catholicism, his willingness to attack church rates in England and the established Protestant Church in Ireland, his silence when magnates attacked trade unions and his 'rabble-rousing' speeches in the provinces. Gladstone was neither a demagogue nor a democrat, but at times could convey a strong impression that he might easily become both. His obstinacy over the Bill led many landed magnates 'to regard him as little more than a prisoner of the democratic movement (**144,** ch. 4).

The extent to which the Bill had divided the Liberal party was revealed when, supported by Disraeli behind the scenes, Grosvenor moved an amendment that the government introduce a redistribution scheme before the franchise clauses were further discussed. On a division, the government majority of seventy after the 1865 election shrank to five. Thirty-five Liberals joined the Adullamite Cave and voted against their own front bench. Most of them were Whigs, or sat for Whig-controlled constituencies. Russell was badly shaken, but resolved to carry on. Gladstone was enraged, although he failed to prevent the Cabinet seeking to pacify the Adullamites by introducing a redistribution scheme early in May.

After considering a number of schemes, the government selected one which planned the redistribution of forty-nine seats. Twenty-six of these would go to the English counties, fifteen to English boroughs, one to London University and seven to Scotland. Industrial towns were to get relatively little: an extra member for Manchester, Birmingham, Liverpool and Leeds, plus new one-member constituencies at Hartlepools, Middlesbrough, Dewsbury, Burnley, Staleybridge and Gravesend. A mild scheme, it was designed to placate the opponents of reform rather than to effect a major shift in the balance of political power. The south of England would have remained overrepresented.

The Tories strongly attacked the proposals, especially the failure to take unrepresented towns (with their Liberal voters) out of the counties. Although Disraeli was much more adept than Gladstone in gaining the support of Liberal waverers, it took him some time to organise a common front against the Liberal Bills. His first victory came when the Adullamites put the government in a minority of 238 to 248 on a cynical proposal to add clauses to the Bill for the prevention of bribery and corruption. Twenty-six Liberals joined the opposition.

Gladstone now became even more obstinate and unconciliatory. He was almost completely out of touch with his own backbenchers, whose support was essential if the government were to survive. Irritated at being outmanoeuvred by Disraeli and the Adullamites, he resolved to carry the Bill in the current session. The landed gentry were horrified when he threatened them with an autumn session, in the middle of the shooting season. Meanwhile, the Adullamites kept sniping at the government, springing sudden amendments to the Reform Bill. For a time they held their fire to some extent, since many of them hesitated to bring down the government at a time of financial crisis at home and war on the Continent. Eventually they were pushed on by Disraeli, who organised a meeting of Tory and Whig aristocrats which decided to put an amendment raising the occupancy level and changing the rental to a rating franchise. This would effectively bar lodgers and compound householders whose rates were paid by the landlord.

Gladstone failed to realise the seriousness of this manoeuvre and took inadequate steps to conciliate the Liberal gentry and ensure a government majority. When Dunkellin put the Adullamite amendment, the government was beaten by eleven votes. Thus, in June 1866, the Adullamite-Tory alliance succeeded. Disraeli had triumphed. Gladstone was humiliated and the Liberal party hopelessly divided. Russell was too weak and tired to repair the split: Gladstone was too obstinate and inflexible. The former wished to drop the Reform Bill: the latter firmly refused. But Gladstone was unable to persuade his Cabinet colleagues to agree to a dissolution. They felt that the Liberals would lose seats at an election and thus allow the Conservatives to form a minority administration. Neither did the possibility of a second round of election expenses within a year appeal to them, despite the fact that the Reform agitation in the country blazed into life and demanded a dissolution. When Russell failed to obtain pledged support in the party for a Reform Bill in the next session he wearily decided to resign, and did so on 26 June. The Queen invited Derby to form a government (**144**, ch. 4).

7 Leaping in the Dark

DISRAELI, 'FUSION' AND THE HYDE PARK RIOTS

When the Queen invited Derby to form an administration, a period of crisis followed for the Tory party in general and for Derby and Disraeli in particular. The Adullamites had not really expected their opposition to Gladstone and reform to culminate in the downfall of the Liberal government. They did not relish the prospect of a Tory administration, especially one led by Disraeli in the Commons. Consequently, a number of leading Adullamites and Whigs embarked upon a policy of 'fusion', the construction of an anti-reform Whig-Conservative coalition. Several prominent Tories rose to the bait.

Derby had to be pushed reluctantly into office by Disraeli, who regarded Derby as his chief bulwark against those in the Conservative party who hated him and were out to break him. Both men realised that a coalition would be at their expense, since it would probably be headed by Stanley. Disraeli realised that to join the Whigs in a coalition would risk losing the separate identity of the Tory party. He had not devoted twenty years to rebuilding the party merely to see it meet such an ignominious fate. Not only must the party be preserved; so also must his own position within it. For a time, in order to preserve party unity, Disraeli had to pay lip service to the notion of fusion. Fortunately for him, the Adullamites played for too high stakes, seeking a disproportionate share of posts in any projected coalition government. Derby quickly backed away from the Whigs, taking majority Conservative opinion with him. If fusion had taken place, there would have been no 1867 Reform Act. As it was, a purely Conservative government was formed. Disraeli, still leader in the Commons, breathed again (**145,** ch. 2).

In a minority of 290 against 360 Whigs, Liberals and Radicals, the Tory government was faced with dramatic events. Not only was there a cholera epidemic, but there occurred the Hyde Park riots late in July. They were mild enough compared with riots earlier in the century, but brought back a possibility of violence unless Reform were granted. The defeat of the Liberal Bill united the Reform League and Reform Union behind a wave of protests and demonstrations in both the capital and the provinces. The Hyde Park riots took place when the League insisted on forcing entry to the park, although the Home Secretary had forbidden it to hold meetings there. An intense crush and a great deal of confusion led to pressure against the delapidated railings, which collapsed. There was some skirmishing between the police and rougher sections of the crowd. The Reform League hastily accepted a government ban on further Hyde Park meetings (**146**).

There had been no bloody violence on a large scale, a fact much bemoaned by Karl Marx. The violence which did take place had not been planned by the Reform League leaders, who were anxious to convey an impression of working-class restraint and respect for law and order. The gap between the 'constitutionalist' League leaders and the 'mob' section of the rioters was too great for a potentially nasty situation to develop into a potentially revolutionary one. Nevertheless, many people were frightened. Matthew Arnold, who later revealed his fears in *Culture and Anarchy* (1868), is a celebrated example.

In the autumn of 1866 a series of reform demonstrations, inspired by Bright, were held in the north of England. Agitation was supplemented as an unsettling influence by other troubles: agrarian distress, Fenian incidents, the Governor Eyre controversy after a native rebellion in Jamaica, and the Sheffield trade union 'outrages'. The need for a settlement of the reform question thus became more acute, when the lower classes were willing to demonstrate, perhaps violently, for a 'genuine' Reform Bill.

EXTINGUISHING GLADSTONE & CO.

At the height of the crisis over the Reform Bill in 1867, Disraeli claimed that his motive in accepting radical amendments to the Reform Bill was 'to destroy the present agitation and extinguish Gladstone & Co'. As far as Disraeli himself was concerned, there is little doubt that the second aim was more important than the first. He was little influenced by the riots and demonstrations of 1866 and certainly did not suggest a Reform Bill in response to them. Disraeli had no interest in reform as such. He saw the question essentially as an instrument for aggravating divisions in the Liberal party, for cutting Gladstone down to size, for consolidating moderate middle-class opinion behind the Conservative party, for keeping the Tory government in power and, above all, for maintaining and strengthening his own leadership and status within the party (**147,** ch. 21; **157,** introduction).

These reasons of political expediency eventually led Disraeli to regard reform as a question which could not be quietly dropped. At first Derby and he said little on the question. They had gained office, although in a minority, because the Liberals had split on the reform issue. The temptation now was to mark time on the question, while Liberal divisions sank deeper, perhaps under pressure from Bright.

Derby resisted the temptation. He calculated that unless the Tories showed themselves willing to attempt major legislation, the ministry would remain nothing more than a stopgap until the Liberals regained some degree of unity. Moreover, Derby was more susceptible than Disraeli to the agitation in the country, whose strength made the reform issue difficult to avoid. In any case, Derby reckoned, that whilst Whigs and Liberals would probably reject another attempt by Gladstone to deal with the question for fear that it might associate them too much with agitation and disorder, they might support a Tory attempt at a settlement. They might feel that a Conservative government was a better bet to resist revolutionary political change than was Gladstone. The possibility of, as it were, a sort of unofficial fusion on reform might lead to a permanent revival of Tory party fortunes and further dissensions in the Liberal camp. In addition, Queen Victoria was frightened by the agitation and pressed for a settlement on reform (**145,** ch. 3; **144,** ch. 5).

Whilst Derby was willing to take the initiative on reform, Disraeli dragged his feet. He feared for the moment that a Conservative Bill might have the opposite effect: dividing the Tories and uniting the Liberals. He was soon persuaded to abandon this view, although he still showed no great enthusiasm for a drastic measure. On 8 November 1866, Derby and Disraeli persuaded the Cabinet to agree to resolutions for the consideration of a Reform Bill. Meanwhile Disraeli embarked on what he called the 'Serbonian bog' by collecting statistics on the existing representation and on the effects of various franchises, statistics which he was to use in devastating fashion when bamboozling both supporters and opponents in 1867.

At first he toyed with the idea of household suffrage in the boroughs, carefully hedged by plural voting, where electors had a number of votes in proportion to the property they owned. When the 1867 session opened, everyone assumed that the government intended to introduce a Bill, although Disraeli had intended only to appoint a commission on reform. Disraeli was obliged to justify the general assumption and dropped his commission plan.

Derby and Disraeli resolved to have household suffrage as the basis of their Bill, since it was a clear and attractive formula. Plural voting, they hoped, would modify its impact. On the same afternoon as Disraeli was due to describe his proposed Bill to the Commons, both Cranborne and Carnarvon threatened resignation from the government unless household suffrage were abandoned. Disraeli nonchalantly replaced it by a £6 rating borough franchise. Criticism by Gladstone of Tory tactics and unrest amongst Tory backbenchers forced Disraeli to abandon the £6 rating proposal as too unlikely to lead to a permanent settlement. He was therefore thrown back on his original plan of household suffrage. Its effect was to be limited by three years residence and personal payment of rates. Despite these safeguards, this proved too much for Peel, Cranborne and Carnarvon, who resigned from the administration.

As in 1866, there were prolonged wrangles at Cabinet level on the details of the Bill, since the complex and varied patterns of rate-paying, tenancies and valuations left room for interminable argument. However, unlike Gladstone in the previous year, Disraeli took great care to remain in close contact with his backbenchers. By taking them into his confidence and retaining the household suffrage basis of the Bill, Disraeli was able to isolate Cranborne, Carnarvon and Peel and nip in the bud any Tory version of the Liberal Adullamites [**doc. 24a**].

Disraeli's confidence was boosted by the low morale of the Liberal opposition. The split of 1866 had not been healed; indeed it had been widened by Bright and the Reform demonstrations in the summer and autumn, when the Radicals had bitterly castigated the Whigs and Adullamites. Dispirited, Gladstone waited rather passively to see what Disraeli would do. His spirits rose when the government's vague resolutions outraged both wings of the Liberal party and restored some degree of unity. At the same time, Gladstone sensed danger, above all the possibility that radicals might tacitly agree to keep Disraeli in office, in the hope that his Bill might be amended in a radical manner. This would avoid a dissolution and leave the Whigs powerless to block reform as they had done in 1866. Naturally, Gladstone was unable to endorse such tactics, which would both enable the Tories to pose as the party of reform and also consolidate Disraeli's position as leader. Realising that Disraeli might ultimately be persuaded to abandon the safeguards against the effect of household suffrage, Gladstone produced his own alternative formula: a £5 annual rental qualification in the boroughs.

THE PASSING OF THE 1867 BILL

Disraeli introduced the Bill on 18 March. In the boroughs there was to be household suffrage, limited by two years residence and personal payment of rates. Thus nearly half a million compounders, who paid their rates through their landlords, were to be excluded. Property owners had plural votes and there were to be 'fancy franchises' for those having £50 savings or paying 20s in direct taxation. In the counties, the occupancy franchise was reduced from £50 to £15. Fifteen seats were to be redistributed.

It was a strictly limited proposal, which would have enfranchised only about 400,000. Disraeli was able to argue with uncharacteristic sincerity that the Bill, while it sought to extend 'a liberal measure of popular privileges' was not an attempt 'to confer democratic rights'. Personal payment of rates was a safeguard against democracy: 'We do not, however, live—and I trust it will never be the fate of this country to live—under a democracy.' Gladstone took the Bill to pieces in deadly fashion, pointing out a multitude of anomalies, drawing attention to Disraeli's unreliable statistics, to the 'class legislation' of plural voting, to the fact that compounders would have to pay a higher rate—in effect a fine—if they wished to pay rates personally and gain the franchise. Yet the very fierceness of Gladstone's assault caused Tory waverers to rally to Disraeli. Even many radicals were fearful lest Gladstone bring down the government and revert to the situation of 1866, with no reform at all (**144,** ch. 5).

Disraeli handled matters with deceptive skill, maintaining an appearance of all things to all men. The right wing of the Tory party was assured that the Bill was essentially conservative. Moderate

77

backbenchers on both sides of the House were persuaded that Disraeli would provide a welcome final settlement of the reform question. Radicals were given the impression that a limited measure could easily be amended into a more drastic one. To keep these differing groups satisfied, while continuing to hold the initiative and outplay Gladstone, was the extent of Disraeli's dazzling achievement.

It did not take long for him to realise that the Bill could not survive without serious amendments. The clauses on personal rate-paying, for example, would operate unevenly in different parts of the country, in some places in different streets of the same town. In effect, the borough franchise would be placed in the hands of the local rating authorities. Neither was there a lodger franchise. The essence of Disraeli's approach was to consider amendments with an open mind, provided that they did not come from Gladstone. By accepting radical amendments, other than those inspired by the Liberal leader, Disraeli skilfully aggravated the divisions between the radicals, the Whigs and Gladstone. At the same time, he was able to skate lightly over the defects of his Bill and the inconsistencies of his position. He was aided by the fact that the interminable lists of statistics and prolonged discussions of nice legal points tended to induce mystification, boredom and weariness among many members of the House. To get the question settled, they became willing to accept almost anything.

Liberal dissension was highlighted by the 'Tea Room revolt' of 8 May, when fifty dissident Liberals refused to support Gladstone's plan of trying to change the basis of the Bill to £5 rental borough franchise. They rebelled primarily because they wished to see a speedy settlement before further agitation made manhood suffrage unavoidable. Moreover, they had no wish to go back to the situation of 1866. When forty-five Liberals voted with the government on 12 April, Gladstone's amendments to alter the rating clauses of the Bill were defeated. Thoroughly demoralised, he considered abandoning the leadership.

By contrast, Disraeli was triumphant. Divisions which had appeared within the Tory party were rapidly recemented. Cranborne and his followers were isolated. Disraeli himself was placed in an unassailable position at the head of the Tory party, which now seemed capable of standing up to the Liberal coalition for the first time since 1846. Disraeli's position was now so strong that Gladstone was more or less obliged to abandon his attempts to destroy the Bill and bring down the government.

When the House sat again after Easter, A. S. Ayrton, a Liberal MP, succeeded in amending the Bill so that only twelve months residence, instead of two years, was required for the borough franchise. The atmosphere of crisis was thickened by a renewal of the reform agitation. The Reform League planned another Hyde Park demonstration for 6 May. Once again it was forbidden by Spencer Walpole. In defiance of the government, the League went ahead, held its peaceful demonstration and gained an impressive moral victory. In Parliament, more amendments to the Bill followed. Disraeli accepted one which enfranchised lodgers in premises worth £10 a year unfurnished. This was of little practical importance, especially when further amended so that lodgers had to have twelve months residence. By 1869 only 12,000 lodgers were enfranchised, most of them professional men resident in London. The importance of the amendment was that it undermined Disraeli's principles of linking the franchise to personal payment of rates (**144,** ch. 5, sec. iv; **145,** chs. 5, 6).

On 17 May the crucial amendment was put by Grosvenor Hodgkinson, Liberal MP for Newark. It would have the effect of destroying the personal payment principle by enfranchising compound householders, for it proposed abolishing compounding. To the consternation of many Tories, Disraeli accepted the amendment without a division, chiefly to avoid discussion of further amendments inspired by Gladstone. The effect of his acceptance of the Hodgkinson amendment was to enfranchise 400,000 compounders and bring about genuine household suffrage in the boroughs. Further amendments followed in its wake. The county copyhold franchise was changed from £10 to £5, that of county tenants from £15 to £12. The 'fancy franchises', virtually impossible to put into practice, were quietly dropped. But Fawcett's amendment, to pay legal election expenses from the rates, was defeated. This meant that the Reform League and trade unions were to continue to find election costs a prohibitive barrier to the election of working-class candidates and the formation of a separate political party for labour.

The third reading of the Reform Bill was passed in the Commons without a division, although Cranborne and his followers charged Disraeli with betraying his party by acquiescing in the emergence of a democratic political system which would sweep the landed interest from power. Disraeli could afford to ignore the charge, not only because his present position was unassailable, but also because he knew that the accusation was untrue. As John Bright had realised in 1859, the key to political power was not so much the franchise as redistribution of seats. By focusing attention on the franchise clauses, Disraeli helped to divert attention from the fact that his redistribution scheme was so conservative that it would consolidate rather than undermine the landed interest. The original plan was to reallocate only thirty seats. Disraeli also appointed a boundary commission, composed mainly of Tories, which attempted to protect the landed interest by transferring suburban voters from county to borough constituencies. Eventually, about 100,000 were transferred, although a select committee, forced on Disraeli by the Liberals, modified much of the work of the boundary commission.

The House of Lords did little to alter the Bill. Tories who hoped to amend it failed to obtain the essential alliance with Whigs and Adullamites. In any case, the peers were well aware of the dangers of trying to alter a Bill which had been accepted with satisfaction by the House of Commons, the press and the public. Hence Derby had little difficulty steering the measure through the upper House. Most of the minor amendments which the Lords inserted were removed when the Bill returned to the Commons. The only major exception was the Cairns amendment: that in the big cities there should be three members, each elector having two votes. This was intended to guarantee minority representation, although in fact it failed to do so. In August 1867 the Bill was read for the final time and received the royal assent.

THE SECOND REFORM ACT

The franchise clauses of the Representation of the People Act gave the borough vote to householders with twelve months' residence and to £10 lodgers, also with a year's residence. In the counties, the suffrage was extended to £5 property owners and £12 occupiers. The Act for Scotland was the same as that of England, except that the county occupation franchise was £14 and there was no lodger franchise (Scottish lodgers had voted as tenants since 1832). In Ireland, the borough qualification was reduced from £8 to £4. The redistribution clauses provided for the reallocation of fifty-two seats in England and Wales. Of these, twenty-five went to the counties, thirteen to new boroughs and one to London University, Birmingham, Liverpool, Manchester and Leeds each received a third member, while Merthyr Tydfil and Salford each received a second seat.

Although exact figures are impossible to obtain, the 1867 Act added about 1,120,000 voters to an existing UK electorate of about 1,400,000. Thus the electorate in 1868 amounted to something like two and a half million. This means that in Britain, apart from Ireland, one adult male in every three could vote. Whilst the lodger franchise proved more or less inoperable, it was the enfranchisement of occupiers in the boroughs which marks the most striking advance. About 830,000 borough voters were added; so that about 47 per cent of male occupiers in the boroughs were qualified for the 1868 electoral registers.

By contrast, only 290,000 were added in the counties; an increase of about 45 per cent, compared with 135 per cent in the boroughs. In the county constituencies, the vote was still largely confined to landowners, tenant farmers, middle-class householders and village tradesmen. The existing balance of political forces was not much disturbed, except perhaps in the Scots industrial towns. In the small English boroughs, many of which were still rural in nature, the electorate was not much increased. Here the new voters were still too dependent on their social superiors to attempt to form their own electoral associations and thus create a distinct political force. In most medium-sized boroughs, the pattern was very similar. On the other hand, the electorates of large industrial boroughs underwent a major change. That of Newcastle upon Tyne, for example, rose from 6630 in 1866 to 21,407 in 1872. Between 1866 and 1868 the electorate of Leeds increased from 7217 to 35,510; that of Manchester from 21,542 to 48,256 and that of Bradford from 5708 to 21,518 (**144,** ch. 6; **155,** introduction).

Disraeli's success in maintaining a relatively exclusive electorate in the counties was paralleled by the conservative nature of the redistribution clauses, which did little to reduce existing inequalities. London, the Midlands and the north remained underrepresented. Dr Smith has calculated that 'the South-Western region with 76,612 borough electors had 45 representatives, while the North-Eastern with 232,431 had 32; the South-Eastern with 80,177 had 41, while the Metropolitan with 263,991 had 22'. Wiltshire and Dorset had a population of only 450,000, but sent twenty-five MPs to Westminster; the West Riding, with two million, sent only twenty-two. This situation was to last for seventeen years, until the Reform Act of 1885.

MODERN WHIGS AND TORIES

There has been considerable disagreement on the reasons for the passing of the 1867 Reform Act. What may be termed the 'Whig school' was preoccupied with the idea that political changes came about in response to a changing economic and social structure and to 'pressure from below' (**12, 30, 129, 139**). Many Socialist historians, concentrating on the last point, are also attached to the 'Whig school'. In their view, agitation in the country determined the timing of Reform, if not the actual details. The much smaller 'Tory school', on the other hand, stress the competition between parties in 1866–7 for the legacy of Palmerston and focus attention on Disraeli's political calculations (**152**). Other historians have been relatively uncommitted (**148, 144**).

What was once little more than a difference of emphasis has recently shown signs of becoming a major controversy. In 1965 Royden Harrison, a Socialist historian, reprinted his provocative essay, *The Tenth April of Spencer Walpole*, which argues that historians have neglected contemporary fears of revolution in 1867 and underestimated the part played by mass agitation in carrying the second Reform Act (**146**). According to Dr Harrison, men of property and power became willing to grant concessions on the franchise in order to break up the public agitation, headed by the Reform League and reaching a climax in the Hyde Park demonstration of 6 May 1867, and hence avoid having manhood suffrage imposed on them later. The agitation pushed both Disraeli and Gladstone in a radical direction: the former quickly accepted the amendment to abolish compounding, whilst the latter suddenly discovered the importance of the lodger franchise.

This view of 1867 was soon criticised. In his superb biography of Disraeli (**147**), Robert Blake denied that either the agitation in general or the Hyde Park riots in particular influenced Disraeli, who, motivated by his intense dislike of Gladstone, realised how eager many MPs were to see the back of the reform question. It was not that the farsighted Disraeli discerned the Tory working man on the distant political horizon, but rather that he saw drastic Reform as a means of isolating Gladstone, keeping the Liberal party divided and consolidating his own leadership in the Commons. The Reform League is hardly worthy of mention (**147**). Professor Gertrude Himmelfarb has stressed the influence of ideas, taking Disraeli's 'Tory democracy' very much at face value. She argues that Conservative principles were more attuned to the idea of democracy than those of the Liberals. The unenfranchised classes in 1867 were, as Bagehot realised [**doc. 21**], apathetic and deferent. Harrison's emphasis on the Reform League, trade unions and Hyde Park is seen as a rather desperate Marxist attempt to make a mountain out of a very small molehill (**150**). The application of Tory principles by the Conservative leaders was of much greater significance than extraparliamentary movements, changes in the social structure or economic distress.

Maurice Cowling's *1867: Disraeli, Gladstone and Revolution* (**145**) appeared on the centenary of the Reform Act as the apotheosis of the 'Tory school'. In scintillating fashion, he denounced the Whig interpretation of Victorian politics, which depicted statesmen acting consciously and conscientiously from deeply held principles of faith in progress and concern for the good of the people. Cowling sees politics as a cynical, self-seeking, unprincipled game, played purely for party advantage. Neither Gladstone nor Disraeli had any intention of creating a democratic political system. In order to stay in power and outplay both Gladstone and Bright, Disraeli was ultimately willing to accept almost any kind of borough franchise. Thus the drift towards household suffrage owed little to long-term policy. It was more a chapter of accidents, the outcome of temporary political calculations and the confusion of party manoeuvering. Viewed as 'an incident in the history of party', the 1867 Reform Act cannot be explained as a simple consequence of public agitation, for parliament 'was not afraid of public agitation; nor was its action *determined* by it'. In the spring and summer of 1867 Conservative MPs proved willing to follow Disraeli for four reasons: their respect for Derby (who supported his colleague); their feeling that a satisfactory solution of the reform question would ensure the future of the Conservative party; their eagerness to see the Liberals humiliated and, finally, their realisation that a restricted county electorate and a mild redistribution scheme would preserve the socially conservative nature of the electoral system.

Whigs and Liberals who supported Disraeli did so largely because they distrusted Gladstone's attempts to shift the old Palmerstonian coalition towards radicalism. Radicals who supported Disraeli did so because they felt that the events of 1866 had cast permanent doubt on the ability of Gladstone and the Whig-Liberals to pass a satisfactory measure of reform. Hence public agitation played, at the very most, a minor role in shaping their motives. Cowling admits that some politicians, for example Lowe and Cranborne, believed that a revolutionary situation existed in 1866–7, but he denies that politicians *in office* feared revolution. Liberals, including Gladstone, displayed more fear of the 'mob' than did Disraeli and the Conservatives. Indeed, there was little to be afraid of, since the leaders of the Reform League were not even firmly pledged to manhood suffrage, let alone plotting revolution. Neither did the Hyde Park demonstration of 6 May 1867 make Disraeli a prisoner of circumstances and push him into accepting more radical amendments than he would otherwise have done, as Harrison suggests (**145**).

While Cowling's richly documented description of the passing of the second Reform Act as an exercise in pure politics is a virtuoso performance, criticisms can still be made. The importance of public agitation in 1866–7 is played down largely by a failure to treat it adequately. Trade unions, for example, receive little mention, although their interest in politics quickened after the Sheffield outrages of 1866 and the *Hornby v Close* decision of 1867 seemed to threaten their position. In concentrating his attention on the crucial six months in 1867, Cowling avoids discussion of some fundamental questions. Why had there been such a change in the political climate that the House of Commons was willing to grant a major extension of the franchise in 1867 when the possibility had been laughed out of court in 1848? No doubt part of the answer lies in the increasing deference and adoption of middle-class attitudes by the skilled working-class elite. Working men seem to have been prepared to be truly radical only in economic questions. This much was obvious to Members of Parliament, who were much impressed by the Reform movement's use of what Harrison calls the 'Rochdale argument': that working men had become so imbued with middle-class customs and attitudes that they could be enfranchised with perfect safety [**doc. 19**].

Further research is needed on the causes of working-class deference after 1850, on the reasons why working-class radical attitudes and movements became fragmented in the face of a powerful middle-class assault at political, intellectual and spiritual levels. If this change had not taken place—if, for example, there had been a really determined attempt to create a strong working-class political party after 1850—then it is doubtful whether Disraeli could have been toasted at the Carlton Club in 1867 as the man 'who rode the race, who took the time, who kept the time, and who took the trick'. As it was, the Reform movement provided essential support for the Radicals in Parliament, who succeeded in edging Disraeli into drastic amendments of the Bill. The agitation, it has been claimed by a recent, relatively uncommitted, historian, 'finally forced the issue by intimidating enough members into accepting the Bill' (**144**).

In conclusion, it is clear that, while the sheer complexity of the situation in 1867 makes it unlikely that a final clearcut solution of the controversy will emerge, *simpliste* versions will no longer do. It is now no longer possible to regard Disraeli as a clairvoyant Tory democrat, consistently planning to establish firm links between Toryism and the working classes. Neither can one view Reform as a simple consequence of agitation in the country forcing its aims on an unwilling Parliament.

8 Landing in Daylight

URBAN DEMOCRACY AND POLITICAL ORGANISATION

Few of the intellectual and political elite looked forward to an age of mass politics without anxiety. Literary figures like Matthew Arnold, Thomas Carlyle and George Eliot saw urban household suffrage as a weapon in the hands of anti-intellectual middle-class Dissenters and ignorant, brutal labourers (**137**) [**doc. 23b**]. Members of the intelligentsia looked to education as the chief means of avoiding political barbarism. In Lowe's sardonic words: 'We must educate our masters to compel our future masters to learn their letters.' There is, therefore, a direct link between the 1867 Reform Act and the 1870 Education Act.

Many Tories prophesied disaster. The majority of the Conservative party had not really wanted reform and, once the excitement of the passing of the 1867 Bill had cooled, felt resentful at Disraeli for cajoling them into supporting a 'drastic' measure. Power, they argued, would soon rest in the hands of what the French called *les classes dangereuses*. More immediately, it seemed that borough democracy might damage Tory election prospects [**doc. 24a**]. What support the Conservatives might gain in large towns could well be neutralised by the adverse effects of household suffrage in the Tory-dominated small boroughs.

Other Conservatives were less gloomy, claiming that the immense advantages of the upper classes in wealth, connections and education, would make their influence felt in the political system for many years to come [**doc. 24b**]. Not only was there the tradition of 'deference' in the lower reaches of English society, but there was also a possibility of striking a rich seam of Conservative support among urban working men, a seam that would have remained too deep to work under a less democratic electoral system than that established in 1867. Those who looked across the Channel saw how, under Napoleon III, a democratic suffrage strengthened conservatism and undermined liberalism, a lesson soon to be repeated in Bismarck's Germany.

Both political parties realised that they would have to make efforts to cater for the political aspirations of working men, in terms of constituency organisation as well as legislation in Parliament. Before the 1867 Act, the Tory party had begun seeking methods of mobilising support among the urban workers. Popular Conservative associations were established in the northern districts, as a response to the National Reform Union and the Reform League. In 1867 this work was continued, when J. E. Gorst emerged as a genuine Tory democrat, eager to widen the popular appeal of Conservatism (**161, 163, 156,** ch. 5).

In November 1867, the National Union of Conservative and Constitutional Associations was founded, linking the provincial associations to a national body. However, despite Disraeli's talk of 'Tory democracy', the National Union received little encouragement from the leadership. Too many middle-class Conservatives feared genuine working-class influence on party policy. Artisan Tories were permitted only a strictly limited role in the party, assisting with electioneering and propaganda. Hence popular Conservative associations tended to attract only deferential working men, content to bask in the condescending patronage of their betters. Those artisans who were keen to further working-class interests as such and seek genuine political power and status, tended to vote Liberal. It is important not to exaggerate the influence of the new Conservative associations. They were largely confined to constituencies where the electorate was too large to be managed by traditional means (**156,** ch. 5).

The Conservatives failed, on the whole, to attract the new voters at the 1868 election, other than in south-east Lancashire (**155,** ch. 14, **160**). The Tories gained only twenty-five seats in the 114 boroughs in the UK with over 50,000 population. Thus the Tories were still dependent on the landed interest; sixty per cent of Conservative seats in 1868 were in the counties. On the other hand, the worst forebodings of the pessimists in 1867 were not confirmed. The 1868 election was fought on traditional lines. Little attempt was made by either party specifically to attract the newly enfranchised working-class electors. The main issue was the disestablishment of the Irish Church; social reform remained in the background. In most areas, politics were much the same as before. No working man was elected to Parliament in 1868, and only two in 1874. Only in certain areas were there signs of the emergence of a different pattern; for example at Merthyr Tydfil, where the miners were instrumental in defeating H. A. Bruce, a long-established Liberal MP, on strictly working-class and industrial issues (**159**).

After the electoral defeat of 1868, Disraeli's leadership of the Tory party, never very secure, became even more precarious. A number of Tories looked to Cranborne, whose dark prophecies in 1867 seemed to have been borne out (**156**, ch. 1; **157**, ch. 3). Disraeli therefore abandoned his tentative revival of the romantic youthful flirtation with Tory democracy, which had served as a weapon for Peel's destruction rather than a guide to Tory policy in the 1850s and 1860s. When the propertied classes became frightened by Gladstone's attacks on vested interests after 1868, by trade unionism and by Nonconformist radicalism, they looked to the Tories to defend the *status quo*. Disraeli was prepared for the flight into the Conservative party of sections of the middle class, a process assisted by large increases in the numbers of white-collar workers and the separation of classes in urban and suburban areas—itself largely a consequence of cheap railway travel (**162, 156**, ch. 4; **157**, ch. 4).

He realised that the future of the party lay in the direction which Peel had indicated in the 1840s: an alliance between landed property and industrial and commercial wealth. Disraeli was, therefore, obliged to woo the propertied middle classes rather than the new voters. Peel was the real father of modern Conservatism: Disraeli was the midwife. Tories were too anxious to maintain the existing social order, too involved with landed property, capitalist enterprise and traditional institutions, to welcome working men into genuine political partnership.

It is sometimes pointed out that the second Reform Act proved a stimulus to social reform. Whilst it is true that the Conservatives passed important social legislation between 1866 and 1868 and between 1874 and 1876, it is as well to remember that these reforms were neither the expression of any coherent Conservative approach to social issues, nor a response to extension of the franchise. The first batch of measures, concerned with public health, factory hours, merchant shipping and London's pauper sick and infirm, was either inherited from Russell's government or planned by Derby before his conversion to reform (**157**, ch. 1). Moreover, it was 'safe' legislation, for none of it posed any kind of threat to the existing social order.

Issues which did pose such a threat—trade unions and education—were studiously avoided by Conservatives.

Between 1869 and 1872, Disraeli and the Tory leaders abandoned interest in both social reform and popular political organisations, since neither seemed to have benefited the Conservatives at the 1868 election. In 1872 Disraeli resurrected the theme of social reform in speeches at Manchester and the Crystal Palace, but made little attempt to translate the principle of *omnia sanitas* into concrete proposals, despite the opportunity offered by Gladstone's neglect of social questions. Apart from the fact that he had little interest in, or talent for, administrative details, he knew of the resistance in his party to anything that might threaten the traditional social system or prove an 'intolerable' burden on the rates (**157**, ch. 4).

At the 1874 election the Tories had no positive policy to offer the electors, other than the implication that the party was a true national party, based on patriotism and the interests of all classes (**155**, ch. 10). Few attempts were made to gain working-class votes and Gorst had little support from the leadership. It did not matter much. The unpopularity of Gladstone's government was so great that the Conservatives won the election, with a net gain of seventy seats over 1868. Obviously, large numbers of both the middle and the working classes had voted Tory.

As far as working men were concerned, their electoral behaviour in 1874 was probably more an expression of dissatisfaction with Liberalism than of a conversion to Toryism. It was also the first sign of the 'swing of the pendulum' effect which characterises a mass electorate (**183**). More significant were middle-class converts to the Tory party, a trend particularly discernible in London suburbs and towns like Cheltenham and Salisbury. Plutocracy was beginning to move towards alliance with aristocracy. Party divisions based on class appeared on the horizon. Whilst the Liberals still had many more MPs with an industrial or commercial background, and the Tories still drew sixty per cent of their parliamentary strength from the English counties and smaller boroughs, none the less the basis of Conservatism was less rural and agrarian than in 1868. For the first time since 1841 the Tories had substantial support in the larger towns and possessed major links with urban industry and trade (**155**, ch. 10; **157**, ch. 4; **164, 165**).

The batch of social reforms passed between 1874 and 1876 have often been regarded as a major response on the part of Disraeli to the post-1867 mass electorate. Dr Paul Smith has recently subjected these reforms to close analysis (**157,** ch. 5). Disraelian Conservatism he concludes, meant 'much the same as other Conservatism: empiricism tempered by prejudice'. Tory social reforms were piecemeal in nature and often limited in effect (apart from the trade union legislation of 1875). They were designed to deal with problems which had become so urgent that they could hardly be avoided. Some of them would no doubt have been passed by the Liberals had they been in office. In any case, they owed more to permanent officials and to ministers like Cross, Sclater-Booth and Sandon than they did to Disraeli (**147,** ch. 24).

There is little evidence for the argument that Disraeli and the Tory party embraced fundamental social reform under the impact of the 1867 Reform Act in order to persuade working men that the Conservatives had more to offer them than had the doctrinaire *laissez-faire* Liberals. The Tory party was still primarily the party of the land (**156,** ch. 3). Conservatives differed little from Liberals in their worship of the gospel of individualism, economic freedom and the evils of state intervention. Moreover, popular enthusiasm was conspicuously absent when the social measures were passed. On the contrary, there is evidence of working-class hostility to state intervention. Few working men manifested much interest in social reform before 1914. Working men who voted Conservative did so for reasons of 'deference', nationality or religion, not in order to alleviate the birth pangs of the welfare state (**178,** ch. 1). Disraeli did not respond to mass pressure for social reform; such pressure simply did not exist.

Tory social reform virtually came to a halt in 1876. The last two years of the Conservative government were dominated by the Eastern Question, Afghanistan, South Africa and the depression. As more of the middle classes flowed into the Tory party, prompted by fears of democracy, radicalism and economic slump, so less emphasis was placed on the needs of the working classes, except in so far as they were willing to respond to the beating of the imperialist drum (**171,** ch. 1). Social reform was hardly mentioned at the 1880 election. The network of popular Conservative political associations was allowed to decay, despite Gorst's warnings that it would mean the loss of the many artisan votes gained in 1874 (**156,** ch. 6). By 1880 there was little left of Tory democracy.

When the 1867 Reform Act was passed, rank and file Liberals were optimistic, arguing that working men could be deflected from their narrow class interests and persuaded to support Liberal and Dissenting attacks on privilege (**12,** ch. 10, sec. iii). Yet the Liberal government after 1868 alienated nonconformists by its Education Act, upset trade unions by the Criminal Law Amendment Act, and offended both the temperance and drink interests by the Licensing Act. Property owners became more nervous after Gladstone's Irish legislation, whilst his institutional reforms rallied vested interests to the Conservative party. The result was the defeat of the Liberals at the 1874 election.

Five years later the Liberals were in a much stronger position. The split between Whigs and nonconformist radicals had been healed. The Bulgarian Horrors had brought Gladstone down on the Tories like an avenging angel (**158**). In addition the Liberal party, while unwilling to imitate Tory experiments in social reform, had come to realise the need for changes in political organisation in an age of a mass electorate. Towns like Manchester, Leeds and Sheffield quickly remodelled their Liberal associations on popular lines, enabling working men to play a more prominent role in the operation of local electoral machinery and the choice of candidates (**155,** ch. 7). The basic unit of organisation in these boroughs was the municipal ward or polling district, from which popularly elected committees sent delegates to a general council which, in turn, selected an executive committee.

There were many variations in types of Liberal association before 1877, but the most famous was that of Birmingham, referred to by its enemies as the 'Birmingham caucus'. A product of the political genius of Francis Schnadhorst and Joseph Chamberlain, its immediate origin was the Birmingham-based National Education League. The latter had developed a system of persuading its members to vote according to instructions, thus enabling the nonconformists to gain a majority of seats on the Birmingham School Board. The technique was then applied to parliamentary elections (**167, 168**). In 1877 Chamberlain and his colleagues took the initiative in founding the National Liberal Federation (**166**). Many boroughs subsequently adopted the Birmingham model of organisation; by the end of the year forty-seven English and Welsh borough associations were affiliated to the Federation.

The foundation of the National Liberal Federation sparked off a major controversy. Conservatives and Whigs argued that 'caucuses' marked the introduction of corrupt, oligarchical and dictatorial

American politics. Chamberlain denied the charge, pointing out that seventy-five per cent of the '600' (General Council) in Birmingham were working men. It may be that in the small boroughs the system failed to operate in a democratic way and the 'iron law of oligarchy' appeared. But in larger boroughs the system worked much as Chamberlain claimed. Certainly the Liberals, increasingly a working-class party, were prepared to allow working men a more positive role in local politics than were the Conservatives in the National Union. Viewed from one angle, the Liberal caucuses were a response to the National Union and the defeat of 1874. Essentially, however, they were a consequence of the age of mass politics ushered in by the 1867 Reform Act.

The general election of 1880, which resulted in a swing to the Liberals of roughly the same magnitude as that to the Conservatives in 1874, was a mixture of old and new. It was modern in the sense that it was an appeal to the voters to put one of the two great parties into office. It was also probably the first general election to be fought at a national level, although local issues remained more important than they were to be in the twentieth century (**171**). It was, more than previous elections, fought over great issues. Conflict centred upon Gladstone's mighty assaults on Disraeli's Eastern policy, enunciated in the great Midlothian campaigns (**170**), although some historians stress the economic depression (**155,** ch. 10). In taking politics to the people in an unprecedented manner, only Gladstone's methods were new. The 'moral issue' went back to the days of the Anti-Corn Law League. The Liberal leader, who always harboured strong conservative instincts on many matters, had little interest in social reform, living standards, wages or prices.

Those who, in 1867, had forecast a completely new political world, must have been gratified that so much of the old political pattern survived in 1880. High polls and the carnival atmosphere of electioneering bore witness to the fact that elections still fulfilled functions that were soon to be performed by spectator sport and mass entertainment. Cartoons frequently depicted political leaders as boxers or jockeys. Moreover, elections still provided an outlet for religious enthusiasm. Whilst constituency organisations were more prominent than in the past, national party leaders still had relatively little control over the constituencies. Party conferences did not exist. Neither did official party programmes, outlining intended legislation, as a bait to dangle before the electorate. Not least, the 1880 election marked the last fling of old corruption, at a time when public opinion was becoming more hostile to it.

THE THIRD REFORM ACT 1884-5

After the enfranchisement of the urban householders in 1867, the next logical step was to extend the same rights to rural householders in the counties. There could be little objection in principle, since the 1867 Act had pushed thousands of villagers into boroughs, leaving their fellows in the counties without the vote (**144,** ch. 5). The spreading of literacy in rural areas removed another objection. Reformers argued that the 1867 Act, because of its mild redistribution clauses, was something of a confidence trick. Further major redistribution was therefore necessary to bring the electoral system into line with the changing economic and population pattern [**doc. 27**].

Added impetus to reform was provided by radical discontent with the record of the Gladstone government after 1880. It seemed that the Prime Minister was over-anxious to conciliate the Whigs, viewed by the Radicals as a group of landed families pledged to the maintenance of the old order and preventing the Liberals from becoming the party of progress. Radicalism itself was stimulated by the appearance of Joseph Chamberlain as the heir of John Bright, whose radical fervour was now more or less spent.

In 1872, Chamberlain drew up his first radical programme: free education, Church disestablishment and changes in the land laws. Such a programme marked the beginning of a new assault on traditional landed society, both Tory and Whig. Radical strength became apparent, not only in the fatal divisions in the Liberal party in 1874, but also in the creation of new popular Liberal associations, culminating in the foundation of the National Liberal Federation (**174,** ch. 1). In 1877 the Liberal party became pledged to extending the suffrage to rural householders. The concurrence of Hartington, the last Whig leader, was a sign of the changing nature of the Liberal party. Whig influence was declining, as the electoral base of the party began to shift from the large boroughs to the 'Celtic fringe' and the nonconformist, often rural, areas (**177,** ch. 17). By advocating rural household suffrage the Whigs were not necessarily cutting off their own noses. In 1867 they had been the chief victims of Disraeli's machinations. The old Whig tradition of enlightened government *de haut en bas* fitted ill with democracy. It had been the Whigs who suffered most heavily at the 1874 elections (**115,** ch. 13). Defeat at the polls led some of them to hope that they might regain their losses under an extended country franchise, though they had little real sympathy with popular politics.

Although Hartington and his colleagues disliked the Birmingham caucus and squirmed under the attacks of Chamberlain, the Liberal party succeeded in maintaining a semblance of unity at the 1880 election. This was mainly owing to the fact that Gladstone concentrated his efforts on attacking the Tory record. To have put forward any official Liberal programme would have split the party, especially on issues like church disestablishment and changes in the land laws. Radicals in 1880 were wary of riding the Reform issue too hard, for fear of upsetting the Whigs. Partly for this reason, parliamentary reform failed to get much attention at the 1880 election. Moreover, it was a difficult subject on which to arouse popular enthusiasm. There was no vocal reform movement in the countryside compared with that in the boroughs before 1867. The kernel of the issue was redistribution, the details of which were too boring and complex for popular consumption.

Nevertheless, when the Liberals regained office, they felt that they were bound to assimilate the county and borough franchises, to introduce a major measure of redistribution and to pass legislation effectively limiting election expenses. Only extremists like Lowe and Goschen baulked at this. There was no danger that the Whigs might once again be dished by the Tories. As early as 1873, Disraeli revealed his hostility to further extension of the franchise, when he opposed Trevelyan's motion and also rejected a radical bid to extend the hours of polling in order to allow working men a greater opportunity to cast their votes. Economic depression later in the decade made Conservatives anxious about trade unions' power and the threat of 'socialism'. Borough democracy seemed bad enough; to extend household suffrage to Tory strongholds in the counties would be even worse (**157,** ch. 6). Rural labourers, dragooned by the new agrarian trade unions, might try to exploit the franchise in order to procure higher wages and undermine the legal position of landowners. This might lead, in turn, to a demand for democracy in rural local government, still in the hands of squires at Quarter

Sessions. If this demand were successful it would lead to increased expenditure from the rates on things like poor relief, rural housing and free education. For all these reasons, the Tory party set its face against further parliamentary reform, having no wish to add a lethal weapon to Chamberlain's armoury.

Radical optimism after the triumph of 1880 was soon blunted. The government quickly lost popularity. Gladstone himself failed to provide firm leadership in the House of Commons. Ideological divisions penetrated as far as the Cabinet. Whigs and Radicals were clearly divided on issues like the Irish Land Bill, subsequent Irish coercion and the invasion of Egypt. Time spent on the Bradlaugh affair and in combating Parnellite obstruction and the activities of Lord Randolph Churchill's 'Fourth Party' made it difficult to pass major legislation.

No measure of parliamentary reform appeared until 1883, when the Corrupt and Illegal Practices Act marked the deathblow of old corruption. Public opinion had been shocked at the revelations of royal commissions on election petitions after 1880, which showed that corrupt practices had been widespread at the election (**172,** ch. 6). The Acts of 1854 and 1868 had had little curbing effect [**doc. 26**]. Neither had the Ballot Act of 1872, although the abolition of nomination day made most elections less riotous (though not all, Chamberlain was hit in the face by a dead cat at the turbulent Sheffield election of 1874). Rising ethical standards, a result of economic prosperity and education, began to deem crude forms of bribery both unethical and undesirable (**172,** ch. 2–4). Bills to remove electoral corruption failed in the House in both 1881 and 1882, largely because of Irish obstruction.

Liberals were especially anxious to pass a Bill, not only because of public outrage, but also because unrestricted electoral expenses threatened to price lower middle-class, or even working-class, radical candidates out of the political market. In this sense, the 1883 Act was a logical corollary of the 1867 Reform Act and the mass electorate. Conservatives, anxious not to appear reactionary, supported the Bill. The Corrupt and Illegal Practices Act imposed stiff penalties, including fines and imprisonment, for those found guilty of bribery, excessive expenses over and above a prescribed scale, payment for vehicles, employing voters as agents, as well as other malpractices. It was stringent enough to be effective. The Act, supported by public opinion, soon transformed the character of electioneering and reduced cases of corruption to a trickle (**172,** ch. 6–8; **85,** ch. 14).

In the same year as the Corrupt Practices Act was passed, Chamberlain drew up his radical programme in preparation for the next election, a programme which he was to blazon across the country in a series of great speeches (**174,** ch. 2). Its basis was free primary education; land reform as a means of fragmenting the great estates and multiplying the numbers of landowners and small-holders; financial reform to ease the burden of taxation on the poorer classes and county councils to democratise rural local government. Disestablishment, manhood suffrage and the payment of MPs were longer term objectives. Chamberlain felt that the success of such a programme depended to a great extent upon a Reform Act which would give the Liberals more electoral support in the countryside. Gladstone, though his instincts on electoral matters were conservative, became convinced that Reform was necessary as a means of salvaging what remained of the popularity of the government.

A Franchise Bill was introduced in 1884. Neither the Whigs nor the Tories cared for it much, but hesitated to provoke a serious collision in the Commons. It passed in the lower House by a large majority and went up to the Lords. Salisbury's tactics were those planned by Disraeli in 1880 (**156,** ch. 1). They were essentially the same as those of the Adullamites in 1866. On 8 July the peers announced that they would block the Franchise Bill unless a redistribution scheme were produced, to be carried simultaneously. Salisbury argued that if the franchise measure were passed before redistribution, then the Liberals would have a free gift of forty-seven seats. In any case, a redistribution scheme would take some time to draft. During that period, Salisbury calculated, the Liberal party might disintegrate, or there could be a general election which the Tories might win.

Chamberlain was quite prepared for a fight with the Lords on the lines of 1831–2, although he knew that divisions within the Conservative party made a prolonged stand by the peers unlikely (**156,** ch. 7). Referring to the action of the Lords as 'the insolent pretensions of an hereditary caste', he claimed that 'arrogant and monstrous pretensions are being put forward on its behalf which, if accepted, would degenerate the House of Commons to a secondary and subordinate position'. Chamberlain did all he could to stir up feeling in the country against the peers. Success was limited, although there were the Aston riots in Birmingham on 13 October 1884, when a Liberal mob invaded a Tory mass meeting; Lord Randolph Churchill and Sir Stafford Northcote had to run for their lives (**174,** ch. 2).

On 9 August 1884 the Cabinet appointed a committee, which included Hartington, Dilke and Chamberlain, to draft a redistribution scheme. Dilke, secretary of the Local Government Board and a master of detail, was chiefly responsible for drawing up the draft. Boroughs with less than 10,000 population were to lose their members and be absorbed into the counties. Two-member constituencies between 10,000 and 40,000 were to lose one of their members. The seats made available were to go to underrepresented industrial boroughs, to London and to the counties. The latter were to be divided into two-member districts, except Yorkshire and Lancashire (**175,** ch. 9) [**doc. 28**].

This scheme was less drastic than many radicals desired, but was designed partly to placate Gladstone, who retained a sentimental affection for the old electoral structure, and Hartington, who saw that comprehensive redistribution might mean the end of the Whigs (**115,** ch. 14). Chamberlain disliked the idea of single-member constituencies, since the Birmingham caucus type of constituency organisation was designed to capture both seats in two-member constituencies. But Dilke calculated that multi-member constituencies would allow too much representation for minorities. For different reasons, Salisbury, urged on by Lord Randolph Churchill, endorsed Dilke's plan for single-member constituencies. He calculated that they would allow ratepayers to dominate elections and give more representation to suburban Tories, especially in London. Dilke, on the other hand, felt that radicals would win more urban seats. The 1885 election proved Salisbury a better prophet.

At the end of September, Gladstone and Hartington overruled Chamberlain and commenced negotiations with the Opposition. Late in November, meetings began between the party leaders: Gladstone, Hartington and Dilke for the Liberals; Salisbury and Northcote for the Conservatives. After some preliminary horse-trading, both sides agreed to single-member districts in counties. Some boroughs outside London retained two members, in order to please Gladstone and mollify the Whigs. The deal was finalised at Salisbury's London home: the 'Arlington Street Compact'. The electoral map of Great Britain had been redrawn. It was to last until 1918, and still remains the basis of the present system.

The compact ended controversy over the Bill. Dilke took the redistribution scheme through the Commons in 1885, with only token opposition from the Conservatives. In July the Bills received the royal assent. As in 1867, the chief victims were the Whigs. Their existing electoral strength had depended to a considerable degree on a Whig and a Radical being elected together in Liberal two-member constituencies. In the new one-member constituencies, Liberal voters would have to choose between a Whig and a Radical; there was little doubt about who would normally be chosen.

The Representation of the People Act of 1884 gave votes to house-holders and lodgers in counties, who had occupied their houses or lodgings for twelve months before registration. There was also a £10 occupation franchise, applying mainly to offices and shops (plural voting was not finally abolished until 1948). Thus anomalies in the franchise were largely removed. Before 1884, for example, there were large rural boroughs where a total of about 75,000 agricultural labourers had the vote; but there were about 400,000 tradesmen and artisans without the franchise in urban areas of counties. The 1884 Act increased the UK electorate from two and a half million to nearly five million. In England and Wales, two men in every three were entitled to vote, instead of one in every three (**16,** vol. i, chs. 1, 2).

The 1885 Redistribution of Seats Act aimed to construct new electoral districts of roughly equal size. There had been great variations. Calne (Wiltshire) had one seat for 5000 population; Liverpool had one seat for 185,000. A county division of Lancashire, industrial in character, had one seat for 150,000 people, whilst a rural borough in the south-west had one seat for 12,000. Seats were made available for redistribution from boroughs disfranchised for corruption, from disfranchised boroughs with a population under 15,000 and from semi-disfranchised two-member boroughs with less than 50,000. The 142 seats created were redistributed more or less equally between counties and boroughs. All counties and most boroughs became single-member constituencies, with an average size of 50,000 population. County divisions were now more strongly influenced by urban and suburban voters, something which Russell in 1832 and Disraeli in 1867 had tried hard to avoid. Thus the landed interest, already weakened by the economic depression which drove apart the interests of landlords and tenants, became fragmented (**173**).

The over-representation of the south and west, which had persisted since the eighteenth century, now disappeared. Lancashire, for example, now had fifty-eight members instead of fourteen. London was at last adequately represented. Cornwall's members fell from forty-four to seven. Moreover, the three kingdoms were now represented pretty well in proportion to their population. But some anomalies remained. English and Welsh boroughs with over 15,000 population had one seat, and those with over 50,000 had two. Twenty-four boroughs had two-member seats; some retained them until 1948.

Yet the old historic electoral communities had largely gone, replaced by somewhat artificial new constituencies. The effects were various. A strong stimulus was given to national party organisations, for the old constituency associations were now obsolete and had to be redesigned, a process which usually involved stronger ties with central party organisation. The end of the old communities meant that the emphasis at elections was placed increasingly on national and regional, rather than purely local, issues. The abolition of most multiple-member constituencies meant that pressure for proportional representation declined. As well as increasing the 'swing of the pendulum' effect, the two-party system became more solidly based in 1888 and 1894, when democracy was introduced at a local level in the counties. The creation of elected county councils, parish councils and district councils seemed a further blow to the political influence of the landed interest.

Part Three

ASSESSMENT

9 Victorian Democracy

It is extremely difficult to generalise about Victorian politics. In the boroughs especially, there were immense variations in both the pattern and tone of politics after 1832. The counties were more homogeneous, except perhaps in precociously industrialised Middlesex, Lancashire and the West Riding. Before 1868, one can hardly conceive of public opinion in most county constituencies. Electors tended to vote in geographical units, or deference communities, rather than according to their degrees of wealth or status, or the nature of their employment (**93**). In counties like Northampton, Huntingdon and Cambridge, the eighteenth-century system of 'influence' was preserved, like a fly in amber, until well into Victorian times.

What political conflict there was took place largely in the boroughs. It could be extremely fierce, as was revealed by high polls, riots and electoral corruption. The extraordinarily intense quality of Victorian borough politics was a consequence of the 1832 Reform Act, reinforced by social and economic change. It could be argued that between 1832 and 1885 there was greater popular interest in politics than there has been since. One reason for this high degree of participation was that politics provided essential satisfaction of emotional needs for excitement and entertainment at a time when there were few other satisfactory outlets apart from religion, itself closely linked to politics. Voting at elections and membership of political clubs conferred social status. Political power was also involved. Groups excluded from the political nation in many areas before 1832, including small businessmen, shopkeepers and skilled craftsmen, were able to challenge not only entrenched oligarchies in boroughs, but also traditional landed society outside boroughs. This is why the introduction of a Reform Bill in 1831 led to a political crisis; the reality of the power struggle is revealed by poll books for the 1831 election (**88**). The battle was fought particularly keenly at a local level; in the contest for control of borough councils, for magistracies and for deputy lords-lieutenancies (**128,** ch. 2).

Study of poll books has shown that the electorate before 1868, in the vast majority of constituencies was pre-industrial (**88**). There was some positive correlation between voting and occupation groups, but party allegiance was rarely strictly according to social class. Urban Toryism was always a force to be reckoned with. Millowners, for example, could be divided evenly between the parties (**97**). So could their workers. In any case, industrial society, at least the simplified model of it as a monolithic contest between masters and men, made a genuine impact on the political system only after 1868. Even then it was a limited impact until the major redistribution of 1885 (**13,** ch. 8). Politics in Victorian England had its roots more in the contest for political power than it had in economics. The issue was not so much about material living standards—the 'bread and butter' issues of twentieth-century politics—as about what kind of people should govern and on whose behalf (**128,** introduction).

This almost purely political pattern was sustained by the fact that the institution of property was taken largely for granted. New electors after 1832 were rarely common labourers. Small shop-keepers and skilled craftsmen saved a considerable proportion of their income and became, in effect, small property owners. They were the the backbone of English radicalism and, later, of Gladstonian Liberalism. Their quest for status and improvement, as a prelude to political equality and power, made them less terrifying to the rich and educated than if they had been a propertyless proletariat. The latter, in reality less genuinely revolutionary, existed only in the counties. Hence the panic over Chamberlain's Radical Programme in the 1870s and 1880s.

Benthamite liberal intellectuals, fed on Utilitarian principles and the Liberal idea of progress, were able to embrace democracy for two reasons. Firstly, the deference of many voters was so great and many provincial leaders were so badly educated and socially isolated, that it became apparent that the traditional class would only have to adopt new tactics and policies after 1832 in order to continue to rule [**doc. 29**]. Secondly, their definition of democracy was a limited one. It was based soundly on property, even if they proved willing to support the claims of small property against large-scale property. Even so, the threat of democratic Reform in 1867 was too much for many of them. Mass politics ate at the foundations of the Liberal theory of democracy, put in its classic form by John Stuart Mill, that participation in politics was a method of inculcating moral virtue in the individual. The method could operate only on individuals capable of becoming virtuous, usually by dint of owning property; education came a poor second. In practical politics, this ideal came closest to perfection in the Midlothian campaign of 1879–80 (**170**).

By modern standards, Victorian democracy was undemocratic. Although the democratic principle was accepted in 1867, 'one man, one vote' never existed in Victorian England, even after the third Reform Act. There was a striking dichotomy between the principles of the 1884 Franchise Act and its operation in practice before 1918. Whig influence on the shaping of the Act ensured that it would not mean manhood suffrage and full scope for the political power of the masses. As late as 1911, only sixty-three per cent of all adult males were on the electoral lists (**180**). The 1918 Reform Act was more effective in relating principles to practice than has usually been recognised (**189**). Nevertheless, the idea of property-ownership as a basis for political rights lingered on, in the form of a business premises qualification, until 1948.

Despite the fact that there were something like twenty separate franchises under the 1884 Act, there were still people included in none of them. Among those excluded were domestic servants, sons living with their parents and policemen or soldiers living in barracks. About twelve per cent of the adult male population remained disfranchised after 1884, as well as the whole female population. Still more rigorous was the effects of a complex and cumbersome system of registration, which placed a number of obstacles in the way of adult males otherwise qualified. It was particularly effective in keeping off the registers people who had moved house, lodgers and Scots personal ratepayers (**180**).

Research on Sussex and Lancashire constituencies has shown the importance of local party agents and associations in the ability to increase the number of registered electors (**181**). It has been calculated that about fifty per cent of the five million disfranchised adult males were barred by the arbitrary and outdated registration procedure. Plural voting also militated against the democratic principles of 1884–5. Redistribution vastly increased the influence of plural voters. Before 1885, only 'one man, one vote' had been permitted in boroughs. Voters could now cast their votes in as many divisions as they possessed property. By 1911, plural voting accounted for about seven per cent of the electorate (**180**).

Such anomalies in the franchise did not go unnoticed at the time by parliamentary Liberals. There was a constant stream of projected legislation before 1914, from both the government and back benches. It made little progress for a number of reasons. The unenfranchised groups formed no solid and clearly identifiable economic interest. All too often they were regarded as the irresponsible residuum. Servants were seen as too open to the influence of their masters, an attitude which harked back to the seventeenth-century Levellers. In practical terms, the House of Lords was a major stumbling block to further change in the franchise, as became apparent when it destroyed three bills to abolish plural voting. The Conservative party would not support franchise changes unless, as in 1884–5, there was a simultaneous measure of redistribution. This the Liberals would not concede, for the Conservatives were seeking to reduce the overrepresentation of Ireland at a time when the Liberals were pledged to Home Rule and anxious to retain Irish Nationalist support.

Further parliamentary reform was also inhibited by the fact that it would raise the issue of women's suffrage, on which both parties were divided. It was not much of an issue before about 1905. The question of votes for women was discussed intermittently by Radicals from about 1820, but was not seriously raised until J. S. Mill made it part of his Westminster platform in 1865 and published *The Subjection of Women* in 1869 (**188,** ch. 1). Between 1870 and 1884 there were nine bills put forward in Parliament. None made much progress. The plight of middle-class women in male-dominated Victorian society, which stressed the importance of the family rather than the development of individual personality, cut little ice. Victorians had a much clearer idea than we have of the role of women. Their place was in the home, unobtrusively ministering to the needs of husbands and children, despite the fact that there were large numbers of spinsters in Victorian England. Moreover, it was widely felt that the interests of women were fully represented in the political system by their husbands and fathers. There was no stronger antifeminist than John Bright. Parliament proved more willing in 1884 to enfranchise uneducated and unpropertied males, than to give votes to educated and propertied middle-class women.

Females were regarded as too emotional and delicate to participate successfully in politics. To give them votes would be to encourage political hysteria, to introduce dissension in families and to prompt the neglect of domestic duties. A more rational argument, at least before 1880, was that politics was too turbulent and dirty a business for the gentler sex. Though not often stated openly, there were two other reasons for massive resistance to women's suffrage. One was based on the fact that women outnumbered men. If they had votes on the same terms as men, then they would be able to force 'feminine' legislation, including farreaching social reform and, more important, strict temperance legislation and laws which would make sexual vice illegal as well as immoral. The second reason was a simple desire to preserve male dominance and keep women docile and dependent on men—one of the nastier byproducts of Victorian romanticism.

Much of the mid-Victorian political pattern survived 1885. Election expenses were still high enough to discourage working-class candidates. The ballot was not completely secret because of the method of counting, whilst there was still a considerable amount of corruption in small boroughs; notably in cathedral cities, where church charities were handy election weapons. The fact that constituencies polled on different days, spread over three weeks, made it difficult to run a national campaign in the modern sense (**177**, ch. 1). Whilst social class had been an important determinant of election results since 1868 in large towns like Sheffield, Leeds and Merthyr (**159**), there was still a good deal of voting based on region or religion rather than on class. The links between Nonconformity and Liberalism remained significant in small towns and country villages.

The fact remains that, as the nineteenth century drew to a close, social and political changes were undermining the old pattern of Victorian politics. Working men began to live in more concentrated districts, away from middle-class influence. The middle-class exodus to suburbia continued. These trends were given deep electoral significance by the 1885 redistribution, which tried to make constituency boundaries coincide with class housing districts. The Liberal party was the chief victim of these changes. Middle-class areas voted more solidly Conservative than predominantly working-class areas voted Liberal (**177**, ch. 17). The Liberal party was increasingly obliged to seek electoral support in small towns, rural areas, Wales and Scotland. The decline of Nonconformity, more rapid than that of the established Church, was another blow to the Liberal party. As votes were cast more on class lines, so the strength of the Labour party increased, a process illustrated by the transfer of allegiance from Liberal to Labour of the Miners' Federation in 1909. These trends were not as obvious before 1914, when the Liberals were in power, as after. The twentieth-century pattern of class politics became fixed only after 1918, having been partly created by the First World War, the Liberal party split, the decline of the Irish Nationalist party and the coming of genuine manhood suffrage (**178,** ch. 6).

The spirit of Victorian democracy, manifested in Victorian Liberalism, had gone. The Liberal party in the 1900s differed markedly from that of Gladstone. The old moral issues were replaced by social reform. Politics played a less central role, at least in urban life, than they had done in Victorian England. There were rival attractions: spectator sport, newspapers for the masses which concentrated on 'entertainment' rather than politics, cycling excursions and cheap railway travel. Group loyalties began to replace individual self-expression. Above all, there was the decline of Nonconformity. The fact that the passion which Dissenters brought into politics had its last real fling in the struggle over the 1902 Education Act was a major reason why twentieth-century politics and elections were played in a minor key.

Part Four

DOCUMENTS

The Utilitarian View

Bentham rejected the views of both Burke and Paine and approached political questions from his new Utilitarian standpoint. It led him to attack the existing political system as corrupt and wasteful, dominated by the aristocracy, which he dubbed 'the sinister interest'. His proposals included universal suffrage, exclusion of placemen, annual elections, equal electoral districts and the secret ballot.

Without any outward and visible change in the forms of the constitution—though waste already committed cannot be caused *not* to have been committed—though past misrule cannot be caused not to have reigned—yet may the plague be stayed. To the democratical, to the universal interest, *give*—one might almost say, restore—that ascendancy which by the confederated, partial and sinister interest has been so deplorably abused, and so long as it continues, will continue to be abused: thus you have the remedy: *this* is what parliamentary reform will do, if it does anything; *this* is what parliamentary reform means, if it means anything. . . . At present, the cause of the *misrule* is this: *viz.* the *rule* is completely in the hands of those whose interest it is—their interest, and thence of necessity their desire, and, as far as depends upon them, the determination—that the misrule should continue—the thing required is—leaving the executive part of the government where it is—so to order matters, that the controlling part of the government shall be in the hands of those whose interest it is that good government shall take the place of misrule: of misrule in every shape, and more particularly in the two most intimately connected and mutually fostering shapes—waste and corruption, corruption and waste.

Jeremy Bentham, *Plan of Parliamentary Reform, in the Form of a Catechism*, 1817, written in 1809. *Works*, Edinburgh 1843, vol. iii.

A Eulogy of the Middle Class

James Mill took up Bentham's view of the aristocracy as the 'sinister interest'. His Essay on Government, a powerful attack on aristocratic political domination, regarded corruption and oppression as the necessary political methods of an exploiting 'sinister interest'. Mill suggested the replacement of aristocratic leadership by that of the middle class, 'the most wise and the most virtuous part of the community'.

The opinion of that class of people who are below the middle rank are formed, and their minds are directed by that intelligent, that virtuous rank who come the most immediately in contact with them, to whom they fly for advice and assistance in all their numerous difficulties, upon whom they feel an immediate and daily dependence in health and in sickness, in infancy and in old age; to whom their children look up as models for their imitation, whose opinions they hear daily repeated and account it their honour to adopt. There can be no doubt that the middle rank, which gives to science, to art and to legislation itself their most distinguished ornaments, and is the chief source of all that has exalted and refined human nature, is that portion of the community of which, if the basis of representation were ever so far extended, the opinion would ultimately decide. Of the people beneath them a vast majority would be sure to be guided by their advice and example.

James Mill, *Essay on Government*, 1820 (ed. E. Barker, Cambridge, 1937).

Postwar Repression 1817

Samuel Bamford, a handloom weaver and Reformer, whose Auto-biography is essential reading, here describes the effect of government repression on Middleton Reform Society after the suspension of Habeas Corpus.

King's messengers did arrive: government warrants were issued; and the persons they mentioned were taken to prison. A cloud of gloom and mistrust hung over the whole country. The suspension of the Habeas Corpus Act was . . . of a nature to cause anxiety in the most indifferent of us . . . It seemed as if the sun of freedom were gone down, and a rayless expanse of oppression had finally closed over us . . . whilst to complete our misfortunes, our chapel-keeper, in the very tremour of fear, turned the key upon us and declared we should no longer meet in the place.

Our Society, thus houseless, became divided and dismayed; hundreds slunk home to their looms, nor dared to come out save like owls at nightfall, when they would perhaps steal through bye-paths or behind hedges, or down some clough, to hear the news at the next cottage. Some might be seen chatting with and making themselves agreeable to our declared enemies; but these were few and always of the worst character. Open meetings being thus suspended, secret ones ensued; they were originated at Manchester, and assembled under various pretexts. Sometimes they were termed 'benefit societies'; sometimes 'botanical meetings'; 'meetings for the relief of the families of imprisoned reformers', or 'of those who had fled the country'; but their real purpose, divulged only to the initiated, was to carry into effect the night attack on Manchester . . .

Samuel Bamford, *Autobiography*, vol. ii, *Passages in the Life of a Radical*, 1844 edn., pp. 43–5.

document 4

Britons Never Shall Be Slaves

The Reform meeting at Hunslet Moor was held a month after Peterloo. The crowd of 30,000, including many women, was regarded as 'an assemblage quite unparalleled in the annals of Leeds'.

Two caps of Liberty next passed, one of which was profusely adorned with various-coloured ribands, and round the other the word *Liberty* was printed. . . . On another flag was inscribed *We demand our rights as men. Liberty, Justice and Humanity.* One of the most remarkable and appropriate flags bore the device of a man in irons, with a padlock in his mouth, and his pockets turned inside out, bending under two immense burdens of

National Debt and *Taxation*. At the top was written *A Free-Born Englishman*; and at the bottom *Britons Never Shall Be Slaves*. Another flag bore the inscription *Hunt and Liberty. No Corn Laws*. Another expressed the grand wish of the Radical Reformers in the words *Annual Parliaments, Universal Suffrage, and Vote by Ballot* . . .

Resolutions . . .

5th That the present cruel and altogether unsocial state of things, is the result of a partial, unjust and iniquitous system of representation—a system that, under the guise and pretence of guarding property, has, by levying imposts upon almost every necessity of life, and upon most materials of manufacture and commerce, by passing corn and combination laws, and laws to screen monopoly in machinery, drawn nearly the whole wealth of our country from the best and most useful of men, the labourers and middle tradesmen, into the hands of that sordid and callous race of beings, the dealers in borough and county influence, who are signalised only as the fomenters of the most bloody and cruel wars that ever disgraced the page of history.

6th That the House of Commons, as at present constituted, is a perfect mockery of what it ought to be, that is, the guardian of the labour, property, liberties and lives of the people . . .

7th That a Reform in the Constitution of the Commons House, is not a question of mere speculation, but of absolute necessity, the present corrupt system having nearly produced a disruption of society . . . Therefore in order to put an end to these great and national evils, we deem it indispensibly necessary, that the present System of Electing Members to Parliament should be abolished, and the Elective Franchise be extended to all persons, who are called upon to contribute, either by taxes or servitude, to the support and protection of the State—and for the better preserving the source of Law and Power *pure*, that Elections be taken by the Ballot Annually . . .

Report of the Meeting held on Hunslet Moor, 20 September 1819.
(Library of the Thoresby Society.)

The Representation of Industrial Interests

The first extract [a] is from a manifesto on behalf of John Marshall, a Leeds flax-spinner, who was elected as a member for Yorkshire in 1826. Passage [b] is from a speech by Brougham, one of the more radical of the Whig leaders, who was elected for Yorkshire in 1830, largely by the efforts of the manufacturers and merchants of the West Riding against the landed interests, headed by Earl Fitzwilliam.

[a] ... shall we not unanimously support a MANUFACTURER, who has passed his life, and earned his fortune, amongst us,—who knows all our interests as well as a weaver knows his shuttle—who is acquainted with the Woollen Trade, and the Linen Trade, and the Iron Trade,—who knows what we expend and what we earn, what we suffer and what we need—who knows the *price of bread* and the rate of wages, and who will do his best to *take off the Bread Tax* and to lighten *the other taxes* as well as to suppress the Rotten Boroughs, and give the Manufacturing and Commercial Interest a fair share in the National Representation?

Speeches and Addresses of the Candidates for the Representation of the County of York, Leeds 1826, pp. 62–4.

[b] Nothing can be more fit than that the great manufacturing and commercial interests of this great country should have a Representative of their own choice to do their business in Parliament. We don't live in the days of Barons, thank God—we live in the days of Leeds, of Bradford, of Halifax, and of Huddersfield—we live in the days when men are industrious and desire to be free; and not when they are lazy and indolent, and deserve to be trampled upon and dominated over; therefore you are bound to have your rights, and to choose your representatives.

Leeds Mercury, 27 July 1830

Russell Takes Soundings

Lord John Russell wrote to Edward Baines, editor of the Leeds Mercury *and leader of local middle-class radicals, asking him about the effects of a £10 franchise in Leeds. The news that the working class would be largely excluded was reassuring. Baines obtained his information from thirty canvassers who had worked for the Liberals at the 1831 election.*

... that canvassers stated *unanimously*, that the £10 qualification did not admit to the exercise of the elective franchise a single person who might not safely and wisely be enfranchised; that they were surprised to find how few comparatively would be allowed to vote. ... It appeared that in the parts occupied chiefly by the working classes, not one householder in fifty would have a vote. In the streets principally occupied by shops, almost every householder had a vote. ... In the township of Holbeck, containing 11,000 inhabitants, chiefly of the working classes, but containing several mills, dye-houses, public houses, and respectable dwellings, there are only 150 voters. ... Out of 140 householders, heads of families, working in the mill of Messrs Marshall and Co., there are *only two* who will have votes. ... Out of 160 or 170 householders in the mill of Messrs O. Willans and Sons, Holbeck, there is *not one* vote; Out of about 100 householders in the employment of Messrs Taylor and Wordsworth, machine makers,—the highest class of mechanics,—*only one* has a vote. It appeared that of the working classes, not more than one in fifty would be enfranchised by the Bill. ...

... there will be in the borough of Leeds, the population of which is 124,000, the number of 6,683 voters. Making the deduction for female householders and uninhabited houses, and persons disqualified by the obligation to pay rates and taxes, I should think the number of voters will be reduced to less than 5,000. ... I need not remark to your Lordship, that if the proportion of voters is comparatively so small in such a town as Leeds, it must be still smaller in less populous places.

Edward Baines to Lord John Russell, 7 November 1831.
E. Baines, jnr., *Life of Edward Baines*, 2nd edn., 1859, pp. 129–31.

Reform, That You May Preserve

The most brilliant speech in defence of the Reform Bill was delivered in the debate on 2 March 1831 by the young Macaulay, later the great Whig historian. Ironically, he represented the rotten borough of Calne.

[The Ministers'] principle is plain, rational and consistent. It is this—to admit the middle classes to a large and direct share in the representation, without any violent shock to the institutions of our country. . . . I say, sir, that there are countries in which the condition of the labouring-classes is such that they may safely be intrusted with the right of electing members of the Legislature. If the labourers of England were in that state in which I, from my soul, wish to see them—if employment were always plentiful, wages always high, food always cheap— if a large family were considered not as an incumbrance but as a blessing—the principal objections to universal suffrage would, I think, be removed. . . . But, unhappily, the lower orders in England, and in all old countries, are occasionally in a state of great distress. . . . We know what effect distress produces, even on people more intelligent than the great body of the labouring-classes can possibly be. We know that it makes even wise men irritable, unreasonable and credulous; eager for immediate relief, heedless of remote consequences . . . that it blunts their judgment, that it enflames their passions, that it makes them prone to believe those who flatter them and to distrust those who would serve them. . . .

I hold it to be clearly expedient that, in a country like this, the right of suffrage should depend on a pecuniary qualification. Every argument, sir, which would induce me to oppose universal suffrage, induces me to support the measure which is now before us. I oppose universal suffrage because I think it would produce a destructive revolution. I support this measure, because I am sure that it is our best security against a revolution. . . .

I support this measure as a measure of reform; but I support it still more as a measure of conservation. That we may exclude those whom it is necessary to exclude, we must admit those whom it may be safe to admit. At present we oppose the schemes of revolutionists with only one half, with only one quarter of our proper force. We say, and we say justly, that it is not by mere numbers, but by property and intelligence, that the nation ought to be governed. Yet, saying this, we exclude from all share in the government vast masses of property and intelligence, vast numbers of those who are most interested in preserving tranquillity and who know best how to preserve it. We do more. We drive over to the side of revolution those whom we shut out from power. Is this a time when the cause of law and order can spare one of its natural allies?

Turn where we may—within, around—the voice of great events is proclaiming to us, 'Reform, that you may preserve'. . . . Pronounce in a manner worthy of the expectation with which this great debate has been anticipated, and of the long remembrance which it will leave behind. Renew the youth of the State. Save property divided against itself. Save the multitude, endangered by their own ungovernable passions. Save the aristocracy, endangered by its own unpopular power. Save the greatest, and fairest, and most highly civilised community that ever existed, from calamities which may in a few days sweep away all the rich heritage of so many ages of wisdom and glory.

Thomas Babington Macaulay, *Speeches, Parliamentary and Miscellaneous*, 1853, vol. i, 12–14, 25–6.

documents 8a, b, c
Fatal to Our Liberty, Our Security and Our Peace

Peel's stand against the Reform Bill was based on the argument that it would destroy mixed government and substitute the tyranny of democracy.

[a] *Debate on the second reading of the Bill, 6 July 1831*
It is triumphantly asked, will you not trust the people of England? Do you charge them with disaffection to the monarchy and to the constitution under which they live? I answer, that without imputing disaffection to the people, or a deliberate intention on their part to undermine the monarchy, or to destroy the peerage, my belief is, that neither the monarchy nor

the peerage can resist with effect the decrees of a House of Commons that is immediately obedient to every popular impulse, and that professes to speak the popular will; and that all the tendencies of such an assembly are towards the increase of its own power and the intolerance of any extrinsic control . . .

I have been uniformly opposed to reform on principle, because I was unwilling to open a door which I saw no prospect of being able to close. . . . For my own part, not seeing the necessity for this reform, doubting much whether the demand for reform is so urgent, and doubting still more whether, if carried, this measure can be a permanent one, I give my conscientious opposition to this bill. In doing this, I feel the more confident, because the bill does not fulfil the conditions recommended from the throne—because it is not founded on the acknowledged principles of the constitution—because it does not give security to the prerogatives of the Crown—because it does not guarantee the legitimate rights, influences and privileges of both Houses of Parliament—because it is not calculated to render secure and permanent the happiness and prosperity of the people—and above all, because it subverts a system of government which has combined security to personal liberty, and protection to property, with vigour in the executive power of the State, in a more perfect degree than ever existed in any age, or in any country in the world.

[b] *Debate on the third reading of the Bill, 21 September 1831.*
But what avails it to retain the name and form, if the essence and substance be lost? Will the Crown, will the House of Lords, continue to possess the legitimate independent authority which the constitution assigns to them? If they will not, they become unsubstantial pageants, unreal mockeries, that serve no purpose but the purpose of delusion . . .

This bill does not violate the forms of the constitution—I admit it, but I assert, that while it respects those forms, it destroys the balance of opposing, but not hostile powers: it is a sudden and violent transfer of an authority, which has hitherto been shared by all orders in the state in just proportions, exclusively to one. In short, all its tendencies are, to substitute, for a mixed form of government, a pure unmitigated democracy

. . . . It is to invert the relation of the people to their representatives, if we are to exclude all exercises of unfettered judgment, all calculation of possible consequences, and to yield without resistance, and against our reason, to the prevailing—perhaps the temporary—current of popular feeling.

[c] *Debate on the second reading of the Second Reform Bill, 17 December, 1831.*

I am satisfied with the constitution under which I have lived hitherto, which I believe is adopted to the wants and habits of the people . . . I will continue my opposition to the last, believing, as I do, that this is the first step, not directly to revolution, but to a series of charges which will affect the property, and totally change the character, of the mixed constitution of this country . . . I take my stand, not opposed to a well-considered reform of any of our institutions which need reform, but opposed to this reform in our constitution, because it tends to root up the feelings of respect, the feelings of habitual reverence and attachment, which are the only sure foundations of government. I will oppose to the last the undue encroachments of that democratic spirit to which we are advised to yield without resistance. We may make it supreme—we may establish a republic full of energy—splendid in talent—but in my conscience I believe fatal to our liberty, our security and our peace.

The Speeches of Sir Robert Peel, 1853, vol. ii.

document 9

Russell and the Landed Interest

In the following extract, Russell explained that his motives in 1832 included the preservation of the landed interest and the independent point of view of the county electors.

At the time the Reform Bill passed, I stated my belief that it must necessarily give a preponderance to the landed interest; and although it may be deemed that such a preponderance has been somewhat unduly given, I still think that a preponderance in favour of that interest tends to the stability of the general institutions of the country. It is my opinion that to frame a plan of reform which should give weight only to the large towns, to the exclusion of the great body of the landed interest, meaning by the term not merely the landlords, but the farmers and the tenants of the country, would be to introduce the elements of general disorder; and I cannot suppose but that those who would be thus unjustly deprived of their franchise would never rest quiet under that plan of government until they had, by every means, endeavoured to reinstate themselves in their due position in the country.

Hansard, 3rd ser., xxxix, 21 November 1837.

Public Opinion in 1831

The following extracts from the diary (1831) of John Campbell, moderate Whig MP for Stafford, shows the impact of public opinion on backbenchers.

27th Feb.   Anything which amounts to the formation of a new Constitution I shall oppose. . . .

2nd March We are quite appalled. There is not the remotest chance of such a Bill being passed by this or any House of Commons. . . . This really is a revolution . . . . It is unquestionably a new constitution.

The general sentiment is that the measure goes a good deal too far. It is applauded by the Radicals and by *some* Whigs, but it is very distasteful to a great part of the Whig party.

3rd March The general belief is that the Bill must be thrown out on the second reading. I expect Ministers will then resign and anarchy begin. . . . I feel inclined as a choice of evils to support and even speak in favour of the Bill.

5th March The measure takes very much with the country.

8th March	I still consider the Bill dangerously violent, but apprehend less danger from passing it than rejecting it.
27th March	The *chance* of the Bill being carried by the present Parliament is the *certainty* that it would be carried by the new Parliament.

J. Hardcastle, ed., *Life of John, Lord Campbell*, 1881, vol. i, 503–510.

documents 11a, b

The New Reformation?

The following extracts illustrate the differing reactions to the 1832 Reform Act of middle-class and working-class radicals.

[a] The Victory of the People is now secured, sealed and consummated beyond the fear of accident . . . the great seal of State has been attached to the new chapter of the people's rights . . . By that Act, a mighty and ancient system of corruption and abuse will receive its death-blow. *The Reform Act* will be an epoch as well known in our particular history as *the Reformation* is in the annals of religion; and our belief is, that its effects in liberating the nation from mischievous propaganda and an unjust yoke, in stimulating its energies, and in promoting its prosperity, will be comparable to those which resulted from throwing off the spiritual domination of Rome.

Leeds Mercury, 9 June 1832

[b] Lay not the flattering unction to your souls, that the Whig Bill of Reform will do you any good, except it prove ancillary to Universal Suffrage. The Bill was never intended to do you one particle of good. The object of its promoters was not to change that '*glorious constitution*', which has entailed upon you so much misery, but to make it immortal. They projected the Bill, not with a view to subvert, or even re-model our aristocratic institutions, but to consolidate them by a reinforcement of sub-aristocracy from the middle classes. The Whigs have too

much to lose to desire *real* reform. The only difference between them and the Tories is this—The Whigs would give the shadow to preserve the substance; the Tories would not give the shadow, because, stupid as they are, they know, that the principle of Reform once admitted, the millions will not stop at shadows, but proceed onwards to realities. Could the Tories have believed that we should be content with the Whig measure, they would have thanked their stars for it as the happiest God-send ever vouschafed to them.

. . . On the same principle, and with a like instinctive sense of self-preservation, have the Whigs manufactured the 'great measure'. They know that the old system could not last, and desiring to establish another as like it as possible, and also to keep their places, they framed the BILL, in the hope of drawing to the feudal aristocrats and yeomanry of counties a large reinforcement of the middle class. The Bill was, in effect, an invitation to the *shopocrats* of the enfranchised towns to join the Whigocrats of the country, and make common cause with them in keeping down the people, and thereby to quell the rising spirit of democracy in England. That this was their object—that they never consulted *your* interest in the measure, will be evident to any one who reads the speeches of Melbourne, Stanley, Macaulay, Hobhouse, and the other leaders of the faction, during the progress of the Bill. They have one and all of them disclaimed those consequences, and reprobated those measures of practical Reform, for the sake of which alone you and we cared one farthing for the Bill! In *their* eyes, its great recommendation was, that 'it would give permanency to existing institutions, and prove a firm bulwark against democratic innovation!!!'

Poor Man's Guardian, no. 72, 27 October 1832. (Philip Snowden collection, Keighley Public Library.)

document 12

A New Constituency Party

The Bradford Reform Society was founded in 1835 as a result of the Reform Act. A management committee of seventy split the borough into seven areas in order to register Liberal voters and organise electoral support. The Tories responded by founding an Operative Conservative Society. The declared aims of the Reform Society were:

. . . to promote by all legal and constitutional means the return of truly Liberal Members for this Borough—to give the Utmost Efficiency to the Provisions of the Reform Act by carefully watching the formation of the Official Lists of Voters and the proceedings of the Revising Barrister's Court to maintain Freedom and Purity of Election, and to Protect the Electors from Intimidation and Oppression, and the demoralising Effects of Bribery and Corruption and to facilitate the Expression of Public Opinion on important Public Questions . . .

MS Proceedings of Bradford Reform Society. (Bradford Central Library.)

documents 13a, b
The Chartists

The six points of the People's Charter had a long ancestry, going back at least to the programme of the Westminster Committee in 1780.

[a] *Address to the People of England, 1838, issued by the London Working Men's Association.*

What, we would ask, but legislation has made the difference between democratic America, despotic Russia and pauperised and oppressed England? If the will of the American people, expressed through their legislature, has raised them from such a poor and heterogeneous origin, to become a nation better educated than any other under the sun—where two-thirds of the adults are proprietors, and while most of the others have the prospect of becoming so—what, we would ask the gentlemen who make these admissions, is there in the character of Englishmen to prevent them from realising similar advantages, were the same political rights conferred on them as on their American brethren?

Granting that a number of our countrymen are in poverty,

can (our opponents) show, by any valid reasoning, the absolute necessity of their being so ... can they trace the existence of that poverty to any other source than corrupt and exclusive legislation? ... America had an adventurous and speculative race to begin with, intermingled with fanatics and convicts from Britain, and for the last half century the poor and the oppressed of all the countries of Europe have sought and found an asylum on her hospitable shores. The greedy speculator, the ruined bankrupt, the broken down insolvent, and the felon pursued by justice, have also transferred their vices to her soil, but her salutary laws and institutions, *springing from universal Suffrage*, have enabled her to reform, instruct and purify the mass, and in despite of that black remnant of kingly dominion —SLAVERY, she is the most prosperous and free of all the nations of the earth.

William Lovett, *The Life and Struggles of William Lovett*, 1876, pp. 174–7.

[**b**] *As a small boy, Frank Peel saw the Plug Rioters marching over the Pennines in 1842, with their tattered clothes and sharpened stakes, singing the Doxology. In the following extract, an old Chartist recounts to Peel the aim of the movement.*

The settled conviction of the Chartists was that bad trade, dear living, and all their misfortunes rose from bad laws, and that if only they could get votes and send men of their own to Parliament they would so order matters that a reign of peace and plenty would at once be inaugurated.

F. Peel, *The Risings of the Luddites, Chartists and Plugdrawers*, 2nd ed., Heckmondwike 1888, p. 328.

documents 14a, b
The Labour Aristocracy

[**a**] There is a schism among the unenfranchised—a schism which, although inarticulate, is beyond the hope of immediate reconciliation. The hewers of wood and drawers of water are widely separated in sentiment and interest from the educated,

intelligent and not infrequently refined fellow-labourer, who is as certain of bettering his condition as the ignorant and immoral are for ever flourishing in the mire, although men and gods decreed that they should rise.

Bradford Observer, 21 November 1861.

[**b**] In passing from the skilled operative of the west-end to the unskilled workman of the eastern quarter of London, the moral and intellectual change is so great, that it seems as if we were in a new land, and among another race. The artisans are almost to a man red-hot politicians. They are sufficiently educated and thoughtful to have a sense of their importance in the State. . . . The political character and sentiments of the working classes appear to me to be a distinctive feature of the age, and they are a necessary consequence of the dawning intelligence of the mass. . . .

The unskilled labourers are a different class of people. As yet they are as unpolitical as footmen, and instead of entertaining violent democratic opinions, they appear to have no political opinions whatever; or, if they do possess any, they rather lean towards the maintenance of 'things as they are', rather than towards the ascendancy of the working people . . .

Henry Mayhew, *London Labour and the London Poor*, 2nd edn., 1861–2, vol. iii, 233.

documents 15a, b

A Hopeless Task

Leaders of the Reform movement despaired of the cause in the mid-Victorian years, when economic prosperity and social changes, as well as the Crimean War, blunted attempts to launch new campaigns.

[**a**] We are a servile, aristocracy-loving, lord-ridden people, who regard the land with as much reverence as we still do the peerage and baronetage . . . I wish to abate the power of the aristocracy in their strongholds. Our enemy is as subtle as

powerful, and I fear some of us have not duly weighed the difficulties of our task. The aristocracy are afraid of nothing but systematic organization and step-by-step progress. . . .

I am also of opinion that we do not have the same elements in Lancashire for a Democratic Reform movement, as we had for Free Trade. To me the most discouraging fact in our political state is the condition of the Lancashire Boroughs, where, with the exception of Manchester, nearly all the municipalities are in the hands of the stupidest Tories in England; and where we can hardly see our way for an equal half-share of Liberal representation in Parliament. We have the labour of Hercules in hand to abate the power of the aristocracy and their allies, the snobs of the towns.

Richard Cobden to John Bright, 1 Oct., 4 Nov., 8 Dec., 1849. (J. Morley, *Life of Cobden*, 9th edn., 1903, pp. 517–22.)

[b] As for Parliamentary Reform, I hold that we might as well call out for the millenium. The Radicals have turned out more warlike than the Tories—what have *they* to promise the country in the way of practical benefits as a result of Parliamentary Reform? . . . No, depend upon it the Radicals have cut their throats before Sebastopol. It is useless to utter their old shibboleths. So you will see that I am desponding. The world will, I suppose, come right in the end, but we don't stand now where we did 8 years ago. The aristocracy have gained immensely since the people took to soldiering.

Richard Cobden to George Wilson, 23 September 1856. (Wilson papers, Manchester Reference Library.)

document 16

What is to be Done?

Ernest Jones was of aristocratic origin, but became a militant Chartist and pioneer socialist. In the 1860s he was extremely active on behalf of the Reform League. Marx was involved in both trade union movements and in the foundation in London of the First International in 1864.

What is to be done with the English working classes? At Leeds they all rise *en masse* because the son of an old Whig lord condescends to address them. At Manchester, Bolton, Nottingham and all about, they unanimously pass resolutions in favour of a £6 franchise *or less*—Manhood Suffrage is not even mentioned, and they allow speakers to advocate measures of reform which, the speakers themselves tell the meeting, will add only 250,000 to the borough constituencies!

What is to be done? If one could hold meetings in Manchester, Glasgow, Leeds, Sheffield, Nottingham, Birmingham, Bristol, Derby, Newcastle, Leicester, Norwich and London, thus one *great* meeting in each of these great towns, pledging the people to advocate and support nothing less than Manhood Suffrage, it might turn the tide, it *might save the future*; but the means of doing so! The men who admirably contribute, the Potters and Morleys and Bathursts and Heywoods, would subscribe to *crush* and not to help a Manhood Suffrage movement. *What is to be done?*

Ernest Jones to Karl Marx, 7 February 1865. (MS letter in Marx-Engels-Lenin Institute, Moscow.)

Transatlantic Influence

In the debates on reform throughout the century, America was cited constantly by both advocates and opponents. Interest in the American constitution reached its peak during the Civil War. The following extract is from a speech delivered at a working men's reform meeting.

They could now triumphantly point to America, and say—see how by the suffrage, and by the will of a great people, the nation has been enabled to pass through the most fiery ordeal that ever a nation went through. They could call on our government and legislature to take a leaf out of the great book across the Atlantic. They could declare to them—You need fear as little that such a course will imperil the throne and the constitution, as the patriots of America had cause to fear that the eradication of the curse of slavery from their midst would overthrow the great republic (loud applause).

Bradford Review, 20 January 1866.

Mill on Democracy

John Stuart Mill was the leading philosopher of Victorian liberalism. Whilst logic led him to support extension of the franchise and the politics of the free market, he distrusted democracy and hoped that the masses would consent to be led and governed by a small educated élite. Hence, in Representative Government, *he warned of the tyranny of the uneducated majority and advocated literacy tests, a taxpayer franchise and plural voting.*

One of the greatest dangers, therefore, of democracy, as of all other forms of government, lies in the sinister interest of the holders of power: it is the danger of class legislation; of government intended for (whether really effecting it or not) the immediate benefit of the dominant class, to the lasting detriment of the whole. . . .

The pure idea of democracy, according to its definition, is the government of the whole people, equally represented. Democracy as commonly conceived and hitherto practised is the government of the whole people by a mere majority of the people, exclusively represented. The former is synonymous with the equality of all citizens; the latter, strongly confounded with it, is a government of privilege, in favour of the numerical majority, who alone possess practically any voice in the state. This is the inevitable consequence of the manner in which the votes are now taken, to the complete disfranchisement of minorities . . . a government of inequality and privilege . . .

The natural tendency of representative government, as of modern civilisation, is towards collective mediocrity: and this tendency is increased by all reductions and extensions of the franchise, their effect being to place the principle power in the hands of classes more and more below the highest level of instruction in the community. . . . It is not useful, but hurtful, that the constitution of the country should declare ignorance to be entitled to as much political power as knowledge.

J. S. Mill, *Representative Government*, 1861.

The Rochdale Argument

In the 1866–67 reform debates, the working men of Rochdale, where Bright had his mills, were cited as the archetype of working class improvement, largely because of their membership of co-operative societies.

I now ask the attention of the right hon. Gentleman and the House to one point which he touched with great force and great beauty of language in referring to some friends and neighbours of mine—the members of the co-operative societies of Rochdale. . . . I will state a little of their case, and I have no objection to rest my case upon theirs . . .

We now come to the Rochdale District Co-operative Corn Mill Society, which does a large business. It has a capital of 60,000£ and turns over 164,000£ per annum. It has also a committee of eleven, but neither the president, nor treasurer, nor secretary, nor any one of this committee has a borough vote. . . . Then there is the Rochdale Co-operative Manufacturing Society, which has more than 1,500 members or shareholders, and a capital of 109,000£. . . . This society is also managed by a committee of eleven, of whom three have borough votes, and two have county votes. But of these five voters only one (a mechanic) is a 'working-man' in the usual sense. . . . Now, the total capital of these societies is 227,246£, the whole of which has been contributed, or nearly so, by the working men of Rochdale. . . .

Now what is taking place in Rochdale societies is occurring in greater or less degree in all the societies, of which there are five or six hundred throughout the country. . . .

You have 1,000,000 electors now, and there are 8,000,000 of grown men in the United Kingdom; can you say that only 1,000,000 shall have votes and that all the rest are to remain excluded? Is the thing possible?

John Bright, debate on the second reading of the 1866 Reform Bill, 23 April 1866.

J. Thorold Rogers, ed., *Speeches on Questions of Public Policy by John Bright, M.P.*, 1868, vol. ii, 175 ff.

document 20

An Enemy of the People

The case against democracy in 1866 was put, with great brilliance, by Robert Lowe, who spearheaded the Adullamite assault. Lowe had seen democracy at work in Australia and was repelled by what he saw. The following extracts are from his speeches on 13 March and 26 April.

The first stage, I have no doubt, will be an increase of corruption, intimidation, and disorder, of all the evils that happen usually in elections. But what will be the second? The second will be that the working men of England, finding themselves in a full majority of the whole constituency, will awake to a full sense of their power. They will say, 'We can do better for ourselves. Don't let us any longer be cajoled at elections. Let us set up shop for ourselves. We have objects to serve as well as our neighbours, and let us unite to carry those objects. We have machinery; we have our trade unions; we have our leaders all ready ...'
... with a pressure of that kind brought to bear, what is it you expect Parliament to stop at? Where is the line that can be drawn? ... for my part, I think Parliamentary life would not be worth preserving on those terms. Look at the position Parliament will occupy. As long as we have not passed this Bill we are masters of the situation. Let us pass this Bill, and in what position are we? That of the Gibeonites —hewers of wood and drawers of water, rescued for a moment from the slaughter that fell on the other Canaanites in order that we may prepare the Bill for re-distribution. . . .
Now, I ask the House again whether with America and Australia before us, and with proof that it is the democratic state of their society and institutions which mainly renders a system like ours unworkable in those countries, it is wise in us

to push forward in a direction which, though it may make the House more popular, will deprive it of the noblest property it possesses, that of working in accordance with the executive Government. . . .

. . . The result will be that the working classes will have a majority in ninety-five boroughs, almost a majority in ninety-three, and more than one third of the representation in eighty-five. . . . It is an old observation that every democracy is in some respect similar to a despotism. . . . As courtiers and flatterers are worse than despots themselves, so those who flatter and fawn upon the people are generally very inferior to the people the objects of their flattery and adulation. We see in America, where the people have undisputed power, that they do not send honest, hard-working men to represent them in Congress, but traffickers in office, bankrupts, men who have lost their character and been driven from every respectable way of life and who take up politics as a last resource. . . . In the colonies they have got Democratic Assemblies. And what is the result? Why, responsible government becomes a curse instead of a blessing. . . . Now, Sir, democracy has yet another tendency which it is worth while to study at the present moment. It is singularly prone to the concentration of power. Under it, individual men are small, and the Government is great. That must be the character of a Government which represents the majority, and which absolutely tramples down and equalises everything except itself. And democracy has another strong peculiarity. It looks with the utmost hostility on all institutions not of immediate popular origin, which intervene between the people and the sovereign power, which the people have set up. . . .

Uncoerced by any external force, not borne down by any internal calamity, but in the full plethora of our wealth and the surfeit of our too exuberant prosperity, with our own rash and inconsiderate hands, we are about to pluck down upon our heads the venerable temple of our liberty and our glory. History may tell of other acts as signally disastrous, but of none more wanton, none more disgraceful.

Hansard, 3rd ser., clxxxii, 1866.

The Politics of Deference

Walter Bagehot, a noted economic and political journalist, published his classic, The English Constitution, *in 1867. He saw the majority of Englishmen as 'narrow-minded, incurious, unintelligent', redeemed only by their 'deference' to social superiors.*

It has been thought strange, but there *are* nations in which the numerous unwiser part wishes to be ruled by the less numerous wiser part. The numerical majority, whether by custom or by choice, is immaterial, is ready, is eager to delegate its power of choosing its ruler to a certain select minority. It abdicates in favour of its *élite*, and consents to obey whoever that *élite* may confide in . . . it has a kind of loyalty to some superior persons who are fit to choose a good government, and whom no other class opposes. A nation in such a happy state as this has obvious advantages for constructing a cabinet government. It has the best people to elect a legislature, and therefore it may fairly be expected to choose a good legislature—a legislature competent to select a good administration. . . . England is the type of deferential countries . . . a deferential community, even though its lowest classes are not intelligent, is far more suited to a cabinet government than any kind of democratic country, because it is more suited to political excellence. The highest classes can rule in it; and the highest classes must, as such, have more political ability than the lower classes. A life of labour, an incomplete education, a monotonous occupation, a career in which the hands are used much and the judgment is used little, cannot create as much flexible thought, as much applicable intelligence, as a life of leisure, a long culture, a varied experience, and existence by which the judgment is incessantly exercised, and by which it may be incessantly improved. . . . So in communities where the masses are ignorant, but respectful, if you once permit the ignorant class to begin to rule, you may bid farewell to deference for ever.

Walter Bagehot, *The English Constitution*, 1867 (Worlds Classics edn., 1928, pp. 235–40).

Disraeli's Apologia

In the following extract, Disraeli was defending the household suffrage Bill against the £5 proposal of Gladstone.

I think that the danger would be less, that the feeling of the larger numbers would be more national, than by admitting what I call the Praetorian guard, a sort of class set aside, invested with peculiar privileges, looking with suspicion on their superiors, and with disdain on those beneath them, with no friendly feelings towards the institutions of their country and with great confidence in themselves. I think you would have a better chance of touching the popular heart, of evoking the national sentiment, by embracing the great body of those men who occupy houses and fulfil the duties of citizenship by the payment of rates, than by the more limited and in our opinion, more dangerous proposal.

Hansard, 3rd ser., clxxxviii, 15 July 1867.

[a] A Dark Future

As in 1866, the chief opponent of the Government Bill came from the Government benches. This time it was Lord Cranborne (later Marquess of Salisbury). He attacked democracy not only in the House, but also in a series of devastating articles in the Quarterly Review. *The extract is from a speech of 30 May 1867.*

We are in danger of drifting into a system of nomination caucuses such as are to be seen in operation in America, and such as will arise when there are large multitudes in each constituency. Wherever the multitude is so large that it swamps every special local influence, that it destroys every special local interest, what happens is the introduction of the hard machinery of local party organization conducted by managers, men who give up their lives to the task,—nor usually men of the purest motives or highest character; and the danger, now that we are following so closely in the footsteps of America, is that it will be into the hands of those men, and not into the hands of those who have hitherto been recognized as the leaders of the people, that the practical government of the country will fall . . . I fear the result will be that persons who are unwilling to shape their every idea and feeling to the test of party—to put their consciences wholly into the keeping of local party leaders—will be entirely excluded from the House of Commons.

Lady Gwendolen Cecil, *Life of Robert, Marquis of Salisbury*, 1921, vol. i, 270–1.

[b] An Even Darker Future
Thomas Carlyle is the most extreme example of those literary men who felt that political democracy would help to bring about a mass culture, which would destroy 'high' literary culture. Household suffrage, he wrote, would mean:

'the equality of men, any man equal to any other: Quashee Nigger to Socrates or Shakespeare; Judas Iscariot to Jesus Christ . . . The calling in of new supplies of blockheadism, gullibility, bribeability, amenability to beer and balderdash, by way of amending the woes we have had from our previous supplies of that bad article.'

Thomas Carlyle, *Shooting Niagra: and After?*, 1867.

documents 24a, b
Two Tory Reactions

[a] I am convinced that we are in a very critical position. Household suffrage will produce a state of things in many boroughs the results of which I defy anyone to predict. In Leeds, for example, the present number of electors are about 8,500. With household suffrage they will become about 35,000.

Is there anyone who dares to say what will be the character and tendency of that constituency? It may be good or bad: but it is a revolution. The Conservative party is in imminent danger of going to pieces now if indeed it does not disappear in the deluge that the Government are bringing on.

Lord Carnarvon to the Duke of Richmond, 11 March 1867 (Richmond papers, Goodwood House, Chichester).

[b] The Reform Bill may be considered 'through'.... What an unknown world we are to enter, but I believe more, or at least as safely, and more permanently than a £5 franchise would enable us to do. If the gentry will take their part, they will be adopted as leaders. If we are left to the demagogues, God help us!

Gathorne Hardy, Home Secretary, Diary for 9 August 1867. (Cranbrook papers, East Suffolk Record Office.)

Why the 1867 Bill was Passed

document 25

Two years ago it was a favourite subject of discussion whether household suffrage was a Conservative or Radical measure. The dominant theory in the regions of the purest Conservatism held a very wide extension of the suffrage to be eminently favourable to the maintenance of our institutions ... The phantom of a Conservative democracy was a reality to many men of undoubted independence and vigour of mind. A vague idea that the poorer men are the more easily they are influenced by the rich; a notion that those whose vocation it was to bargain and battle with the middle class must on that account love the gentry; an impression—for it could be no more—that the ruder class of minds would be more sensitive to traditional emotions; and an indistinct application to English politics of Napoleon's (then) supposed success in taming revolution by universal suffrage; all these arguments, never thought out, but floating loosely in men's minds, and accepted as motives for action at a time when the party battle was too hot to admit of close reflection, went to make up the clear conviction of the mass of the Conservative party, that in a Reform Bill more Radical than that of the Whigs they had discovered the secret of a sure and signal triumph.

'The past and future of Conservative policy', *Quarterly Review*, cxxvii (October 1869), 541–2. (written by Salisbury)

Corruption

Corrupt boroughs survived both 1832 and 1867. The most famous case was Beverley, where the novelist Anthony Trollope was an unsuccessful candidate and recorded his disgust in his Autobiography (1883) *and his novel* Ralph the Heir (1871), *where Beverley is thinly disguised as 'Percycross'. The extract below refers to the 1865 Lancaster election, when £14,000 was spent on corrupting the 1408 electors. In 1867 the borough was disfranchised as incurably corrupt.*

Out of a total of 1408 electors, 843 were guilty of bribery thereat by receiving money or other valuable consideration for having given, or to induce them to give, their votes; that a further number of 139 persons were guilty of corrupt practices at the said election by corruptly giving or promising money or other valuable consideration to voters for the purchase of their votes . . . and that of the said 139 persons 89 were electors and 50 were not voters for the borough.

Parliamentary Papers 1867, xxvii, xii, Report of the Lancaster Bribery Commission.

The Agricultural Labourers

In 1873 Trevelyan introduced a private member's bill to extend household suffrage to the counties. He withdrew it in a thin House. After explaining that the Government had no official policy on the question, W. E.

Forster declared his personal support, after reviewing the arguments of opponents.

Why are these persons to be excluded any longer from the franchise, and why was not their inclusion passed in 1867? I wish to be perfectly candid with the House, and to state what struck me as being two or three grounds for that course not having been taken . . . the first of these grounds was the exist-ence of a general impression that the agricultural or county householder was less educated than the artisan householder to be found in the towns. . . . Another ground for urging that the county householders should not have the franchise before was, that they took no interest in politics as compared with the borough householders . . . There may also have been . . . a fear that their votes could not be relied upon as likely to be given in support of Liberal candidates.

Hansard, 3rd ser., ccxvii, 23 July 1873.

document 28
Compromise in 1884–85

The Reform Bill of 1884–85 was essentially a compromise between the parties, with little debate on principles. This is reflected in the following extract from Gladstone's speech.

We shall seek to deal with these anomalies in a manner agree-able to the spirit of English legislation, not absolutely to efface all inequality from our representative system in respect to electoral areas—not to aim at the application of a single hard mathematical rule, but to give due weight to the various, and in some senses conflicting, considerations that bear upon the question from different points, and to attain that kind of practical result by a change sufficiently wide, yet not reckless in character, and which is agreeable to the traditions and practices of Parliament.

Hansard, 3rd ser., ccxciv, 1 December 1884.

Noblesse Oblige

William Jackson was M.P. for Leeds and had made a fortune from textiles, leather and railways. Balfour's letter to his uncle exudes the assurance of the old ruling class, as late as 1891.

He is a man whom it would be very desirable ultimately to have in the Cabinet and who in the meanwhile would do the post office to perfection. He has great tact and judgment—middle-class tact and judgment I admit, but good of their kind. He justly inspires great confidence in businessmen; and he is that *rara avis*, a successful manufacturer who is fit for something besides manufacturing. A cabinet of Jacksons would be rather a serious order, no doubt; but one or even two would be a considerable addition to any cabinet.

Balfour to Salisbury, 27 August 1891. (Salisbury papers, Christ Church, Oxford.)

Appendix 1: The Electorate

	Electors		Population (in millions)	
	England and Wales	UK	England and Wales	UK
1831	435,000	478,000	14	24
1833	700,000	813,000		
1865	1,000,000	1,430,000	22	30
1868	2,000,000	2,500,000		
1883	2,500,000	3,000,000	26	35
1885	4,400,000	4,900,000	27	36

Adult males able to vote

1800	3 in every 100	
1833	1 in every 7	(1 in 5 in England)
1868	1 in every 3	(excluding Ireland)
1885	2 in every 3	

Appendix 2:
Franchise Qualifications

(Minor franchises, involving relatively small numbers, have been omitted.)

Before 1832
Boroughs: Various qualifications.
Counties: 40s freeholders.
1832–67

Boroughs: £10 property owners. £10 lodgers (if sharing a house and the landlord not in occupation). Most holders of pre-1832 franchises retained them for life.
Counties: 40s freeholders, £10 copyholders, £50 tenants, £10 long leaseholders (60 years), £50 medium leaseholders (20 years).
Borough freeholders could vote in counties if their freehold was between 40s and £10, or if it was over £10 and occupied by a tenant.

1867–84
Boroughs: Householders with one year's residence. £10 lodgers with one year's residence.
Counties: The franchise was also given to £12 occupiers (£14 in Scotland) and £5 property owners.

1884–1918
The distinction between boroughs and counties was abolished when single-member constituencies were introduced. The main franchise qualification became that of the 1867 borough franchise: occupation of a dwelling-house for a period of twelve months before the qualifying date. The lodger franchise and the £10 occupation franchise (usually for shops and offices) were extended to the counties.

Chronological Summary

1813	Cartwright's missionary tour
1815	End of the War; Corn Laws passed
1816	Spa Fields riots; spread of Hampden Clubs in the north
1817	The 'Blanketeers'; Pentridge Rising
1818	Bentham's Plan for *Parliamentary Reform* published
1819	Peterloo Massacre
1820	The Six Acts; James Mill's *Essay on Government*
1824	*Westminster Review* founded
1827	End of the Liverpool ministry
1829	Catholic emancipation; Birmingham Political Union founded
1830	June. Election after the death of George IV
	November. Fall of the Wellington Government; formation of the Whig ministry
1831	March. Russell introduced the first Reform Bill
	April. Grey dissolved; general election
	Sept. Reform Bill passed its third reading in the House of Commons
	Oct. The House of Lords rejected the Bill
	Riots at Nottingham, Derby, Bristol
	Dec. Russell introduced a second Reform Bill
1832	April. The Bill passed its third reading in the House of Commons; William IV refused to create peers and Grey resigned. Wellington failed to form a government.
	May. Disturbances in London: the 'Days of May'
	Grey returned to office; the King agreed to create peers; the House of Lords surrendered
	June. The 1832 Reform Act became law
1838	London Working Men's Association founded. Anti-Corn Law League established
1839	First Chartist petition
1842	Second Chartist petition; Plug Riots
1846	Corn Laws repealed
1848	Third Chartist petition
1852	Russell's Reform Bill failed in the House of Commons
1854	Outbreak of the Crimean War; Russell withdrew his second Reform Bill
1858	The Reform Bill of Derby and Disraeli defeated
1859	Failure of Bright's provincial campaign for parliamentary reform

1860	Defeat of Russell's third Reform Bill. John Stuart Mill's *On Liberty*
1861	Outbreak of the American Civil War. Mill's *Representative Government*
1863	Gladstone's 'thunderbolt of a sentence' on Reform
1864	National Reform Union and the Reform League founded
1865	Death of Palmerston. Russell became prime minister
1866	Feb. Gladstone introduced a Reform Bill
	March. The 'Cave of Adullam' formed
	June. Dunkellin's amendment passed. Russell resigned Derby and Disraeli took office
	July. Hyde Park riots
	Oct. Reform meetings in the north. Derby converted to Reform
1867	March. Disraeli introduced the Reform Bill
	May. 'Tea Room revolt' divided the Liberals
	Hodgkinson's amendment passed, abolishing compounding
	August. The 1867 Reform Act became law
	National Union of Conservative and Constitutional Associations founded
1868	Liberals won the general election; Gladstone prime minister
1869	National Education League founded
1872	Chamberlain's Radical Programme. Ballot Act
1874	Conservatives won the general election and took office
1877	National Liberal Federation founded. Liberals pledged to rural householder franchise and redistribution.
1880	Liberals won the general election; Gladstone prime minister
1883	Corrupt and Illegal Practices Act
1884	March. Franchise Bill
	July. The peers block the Bill
	Sept. Negotiations between government and opposition leaders
	Nov. 'Arlington Street Compact' on redistribution. Franchise Bill became law
1885	Redistribution Bill passed

Bibliography

Documents:
1 Williams, E. N., *The Eighteenth Century Constitution 1688–1815*: *Documents and Commentary*, Cambridge U.P. 1965.
2 Hanham, H. J., *The Nineteenth Century Constitution 1815–1914*: *Documents and Commentary*, Cambridge U.P. 1969.

Both contain excellent bibliographies.

3 Aspinall, A. and Anthony Smith, E., eds., *English Historical Documents*, xi, *1783–1832*, Eyre & Spottiswoode 1959.
4 Young, G. M. and Handcock, W. D., eds., *English Historical Documents*, xii(1), *1833–1874*, Eyre & Spottiswoode 1956.
5 Costin, W. C. and Steven Watson J., *The Law and Working of the Constitution: Documents 1660–1914*, ii, *1784–1914*, A. & C. Black 1952.
6 Bullock, A. and Shock, M., eds., *The Liberal Tradition*, A. & C. Black 1956.
7 White, R. J., ed., *The Conservative Tradition*, A. and C. Black, 2nd edn. 1964.
8 Maccoby, S., ed., *The English Radical Tradition*, A. and C. Black 1955.
9 Cole, G. D. H. and Filson, A. W., *British Working Class Movements: Select Documents 1789–1875*, Macmillan 1951.
10 Nicholas, H. G., *To the Hustings*, Cassell 1956, reprints accounts of elections from contemporary fiction.

Two good textbooks on the eighteenth and nineteenth centuries are:
11 Marshall, Dorothy, *Eighteenth Century England*, Longmans 1962.
12 Briggs, Asa, *The Age of Improvement*, Longmans 1959.

See also two products of a lifetime of profound scholarship:
13 Kitson Clark, G., *The Making of Victorian England*, Methuen 1962.

14 Kitson Clark, G., *An Expanding Society*, Cambridge U.P. 1967.

15 Read, D., *The English Provinces c. 1760–1960*, Arnold 1964, contains a good deal on political movements.

16 Jennings, Sir Ivor, *Party Politics*, Cambridge U.P., i, *Appeal to the People*, 1960; ii, *The Growth of Parties*, 1961; iii, *The Stuff of Politics*, 1962, covers the period from the eighteenth century to the present.

For political ideas, see:

17 Macpherson, C. B., *The Real World of Democracy*, Oxford U.P. 1966.

18 Harris, R. W., *Political Ideas 1760–92*, Gollancz 1963.

19 Canavan, F. P., *The Political Reason of Edmund Burke*, Duke U.P. 1960.

20 Fennessy, R. R., *Burke, Paine and the Rights of Man*, Nijoff, Hague 1963.

21 Derry, J. W., *The Radical Tradition*, Macmillan 1967—useful essays on Paine and Cobbett.

22 Letwin, S. R., *The Pursuit of Certainty*, Cambridge U.P. 1965, has perceptive essays on Bentham and John Stuart Mill.

23 Hamburger, J., *Intellectuals in Politics, John Stuart Mill and the Philosophic Radicals*, Yale U.P. 1965.

24 Cowling, M., *Mill and Liberalism*, Cambridge U.P. 1963. A swingeing attack on Mill.

25 Burke's *Reflections on the French Revolution*, Paine's *Rights of Man* and Mill's *On Liberty*, *Utilitarianism* and *Representative Government* are available in Everymans Library (Dent).

26 Fitzjames Stephen, James, *Liberty, Equality, Fraternity* (2nd edn, 1874), ed. R. J. White, Cambridge U.P. 1968, is the classic Conservative answer to Mill.

There is no monograph on the debate about democracy in the 1860s. Three contemporary works may be consulted:

27 Lowe, Robert, *Speeches and Letters on Reform 1867*. The anti-democratic case.

28 *Essays on Reform*, 1867, by various contributors. An answer to Lowe.

29 Bagehot, W., *The English Constitution* 1867 and 1872 (Worlds Classics edn, Oxford U.P. 1928 and reprints).

30 Briggs, A., *Victorian People*, Penguin edn, 1965, examines the debate in chapter 9. See also: Roach, J., 'Liberalism and the Victorian Intelligentsia', *Cambridge Historical Journal*, xiii, no. 1, 1957. See also **150** below.

The later eighteenth-century constitution is best approached through **1** above and:

31 Namier, L. B., *The Structure of Politics at the Accession of George III*, 2nd edn, Macmillan 1967.

32 Namier, L. B., *England in the Age of the American Revolution*, 2nd edn, Macmillan 1961.

33 Namier, L. B., *Crossroads of Power: Essays on Eighteenth Century England*, Hamish Hamilton 1962.

34 Pares, R., *King George III and the Politicians*, Clarendon Press 1953.

35 Owen, J. B., *The Pattern of Politics in Eighteenth Century England*, Historical Association pamphlet 1962.

36 Foord, A. S., *His Majesty's Opposition 1714–1830*, Clarendon Press 1964.

For elections, see:

37 Porritt, E. and A. G., *The Unreformed House of Commons*, 2 vols. Cambridge U.P. 1930.

38 Bonsall, B., *Sir James Lowther and Cumberland and Westmorland elections 1754–75*, Manchester U.P. 1960.

39 Smith, E. Anthony, 'Earl Fitzwilliam and Malton', *English Historical Review*, lxxx, 1965.

40 Smith, E. Anthony, 'The Yorkshire Elections of 1806–7', *Northern History*, ii, 1967.

The early parliamentary reform movement is discussed by

41 Veitch, G. S., *The Genesis of Parliamentary Reform*, Constable 1913, reissued 1965. Deals with the question from 1760 to 1832.

42 Thompson, E. P., *The Making of the English Working Class*, Gollancz 1963, Penguin 1968, is a neo-Marxist *tour de force*. The reform movement is only one of many themes brilliantly illumined.

43 Robbins, C., *The Eighteenth Century Commonwealthman*, Harvard U.P. 1959, is a splendid study of the survival of the seventeenth century republican tradition.

44 Rudé, G., *Wilkes and Liberty*, Clarendon Press 1962.
45 Christie, I. R., *Wilkes, Wyvill and Reform*, Macmillan 1962.
46 Rudé, G., 'The Middlesex electors of 1768–1769', *English Historical Review*, lxxv, 1960.
47 Rudé, G., 'The London "mob" of the eighteenth century', *Historical Journal*, ii, no. 1, 1959.
48 Christie, I. R., 'The Yorkshire Association 1780–84', *Historical Journal*, ii, no. 3, 1960.
49 Phillips, N. C., 'Edmund Burke and the county movement 1779–1780', *English Historical Review*, lxxvi, 1961.
50 Black, E. C., *The Association: British Extra-Parliamentary Organisation 1769–1793*, Harvard U.P. 1963.
51 Maccoby, S., *English Radicalism 1762–1785*, Allen & Unwin 1955.
52 Cobban, A., *The Debate on the French Revolution*, Kaye 1950.
53 Brown, P. A., *The French Revolution in English History*, 1918, reissue Cass 1965.
54 O'Gorman, F., *The Whig Party and the French Revolution*, Macmillan 1967.
55 Williams, G. A., *Artisans and Sansculottes*, Arnold 1968.
56 Collins, H., 'The London Corresponding Society' in J. Saville, ed., *Democracy and the Labour Movement*, Lawrence & Wishart 1954.
57 Ginter, D. C., 'The Loyalist Association Movement 1792–3 and British Public Opinion', *Historical Journal*, ix, no. 2, 1966.
58 Taylor, J., 'The Sheffield Constitutional Society 1791–95', *Transactions of the Hunter Archaeological Society*, v, 1938–43.
59 Seaman, A. W. L., 'Reform politics in Sheffield 1791–97', *ibid.*, vii, 1951.
60 Handforth, P., 'Manchester radical politics 1789–94', *Trans. of the Lancs. and Cheshire Antiquarian Society*, lxvi, 1956.
61 Miller, N. C., 'John Cartwright and radical parliamentary reform 1808–1819', *English Historical Review*, lxxxiii, 1968.

For postwar Reform politics see above, **15, 41, 42, 61,** and:

62 White, R. J., *Waterloo to Peterloo*, Heinemann 1957, a Tory version, worth comparing with **42** above.
63 Read, D., *Press and People 1790–1850*, Arnold 1961.
64 Read, D., *Peterloo: the Massacre and its Background*, Manchester U.P. 1958.

65 Temple Patterson, A., 'Luddism, Hampden Clubs and trade unions in Leicestershire 1816–1817', *English Historical Review*, lxiii, 1948.

66 Wallas, G., *Life of Francis Place*, Fisher Unwin 1898.

67 Williams, G. A., *Rowland Detrosier. A Working Class Infidel 1800–34*, St Anthony's Press, York, 1965.

68 Chaloner, W. H., ed., *Autobiography of Samuel Bamford*, vol. ii, *Passages in the Life of a Radical*, Cass 1967. A classic account which first appeared in 1843.

69 Mitchell, A. V., *The Whigs in Opposition 1815–30*, Clarendon Press 1967.

70 Fraser, P., 'Public petitioning and Parliament before 1932', *History*, xlvii, 158, 1961.

71 Briggs, A., 'Middle class consciousness in English politics 1780–1846', *Past and Present*, ix, 1956.

72 Main, J. M., 'Working class politics in Manchester from Peterloo to the Reform Act', *Historical Studies of Australia and New Zealand*, vi, 1955.

The Reform crisis of 1828–32 is dealt with in:

73 Machin, G. I. T., *The Catholic Question in English Politics 1820–30*, Clarendon Press 1964, see also **69** above.

74 Butler, J. R. M., *The Passing of the Great Reform Bill*, Longmans 1914; reissue Cass 1964. The standard account.

75 Maehl, W. H., ed., *The Reform Bill of 1832*, Holt, Rinehart, Winston 1967. An edited selection of historians' versions of 1832, with a commentary and useful bibliography.

76 Briggs, A., 'The background of the parliamentary reform movement in three English cities', *Cambridge Historical Journal*, iii, 1952, is a key article.

77 Moore, D. C., 'The other face of reform', *Victorian Studies*, v, 1961 is also compulsory reading.

78 Moore, D. C., 'Concession or cure: the sociological premises of the first Reform Act', *Historical Journal*, ix, 1966.

79 Bradfield, B. T., 'Sir Richard Vyvyan and the country gentlemen 1830–34', *English Historical Review*, lxxxiii, 1968.

80 Ferguson, H., 'The Birmingham Political Union and the Government 1831–2', *Victorian Studies*, iii, no. 3, 1960.

81 Rudé, G., 'English rural and urban disturbances 1830–1', *Past and Present*, xxxvii, 1967.

82 Temple Patterson, A., *Radical Leicester*, University College, Leicester, 1954.

83 Hamburger, J., *James Mill and the Art of Revolution*, Yale U.P. 1963.

84 Mather, F. C., *Public Order in the Age of the Chartists*, Manchester U.P. 1959.

The effects of the 1832 Reform Act can be studied in **13** and **14** above, and:

85 Seymour, C., *Electoral Reform in England and Wales 1832–1885*, Yale U.P. 1915.

86 Gash, N., *Politics in the Age of Peel*, Longmans 1953, is an elegant and scholarly description of the reformed electoral system.

87 Gash, N., *Reaction and Reconstruction in English Politics 1832–52*, Clarendon Press 1965.

88 Vincent, J. R., *Pollbooks: How the Victorians Voted*, Cambridge U.P. 1967.

89 Gwyn, W. B., *Democracy and the Cost of Politics*, Athlone Press 1962.

90 Kitson Clark, G., *Peel and the Conservative Party*, Bell 1929; 2nd edn, Cass 1964.

91 McCord, N., 'Some difficulties of parliamentary reform', *Historical Journal*, x, no. 3, 1967.

92 Ferguson, W., 'The Reform Act (Scotland) of 1832: intention and effect', *Scottish Historical Review*, xlv, 1966.

93 Moore, D. C., 'Social structure, political structure and public opinion in mid-Victorian England', in R. Robson, ed., *Ideas and Institutions of Victorian Britain*, Bell 1967.

94 Thompson, F. M. L., 'Whigs and Liberals in the West Riding 1830–1860', *English Historical Review*, lxxiv, 1959.

95 Vincent, J. R., 'The electoral sociology of Rochdale', *Economic History Review*, 2nd ser., xvi, 1963.

96 McCord, N., 'Post-reform politics in Gateshead', *Northern History*, iv, 1969.

97 Wright, D. G., 'A radical borough: parliamentary politics in Bradford 1832–41', *Northern History*, iv, 1969.

98 Golby, J., 'A great electioneer and his motives', *Historical Journal*, viii, no. 2, 1965.

99 Temple Patterson, A., 'Electoral corruption in early Victorian Leicester', *History*, xxxi, 114, 1946.

100 Thomas, J. A., 'The System of Registration and the Development of Party Organisation 1832–70', *History*, xxxv, 1950.

101 Woolley, S. F., 'The Personnel of the Parliament of 1833', *English Historical Review*, liii, 1938.

102 Ransome, M., 'Some recent studies in the composition of the House of Commons', *Birmingham Historical Journal*, vi, no. 2, 1958.

103 Aydelotte, W. O., 'The House of Commons in the 1840s', *History*, xxxix, 1954.

104 Salter, F. R., 'Political nonconformity in the 1830s', *Transactions of the Royal Historical Society*, 5th ser., iii, 1953.

There is no adequate standard account of Chartism, but see:

105 Hovell, M., *The Chartist Movement*, 3rd edn, Manchester U.P. 1966.

106 Briggs, A., ed., *Chartist Studies*, Macmillan 1959.

107 Mather, F. C., *Chartism*, Historical Association pamphlet G61, 1965.

108 Cole, G. D. H., *Chartist Portraits*, Macmillan 1941, reissued 1965.

109 Harrison, B. and Hollis, P., 'Chartism, Liberalism and the life of Robert Lowery', *English Historical Review*, lxxxii, 1967.

The Corn Law crisis is discussed by:

110 Kitson Clark, G., 'The electorate and the repeal of the Corn Laws', *Trans. Royal Historical Society*, 5th ser., i, 1951.

111 Kemp, B., 'Reflections on the repeal of the Corn Laws', *Victorian Studies*, v, no. 3, 1962.

112 Aydelotte, W. O., 'The country gentlemen and the repeal of the Corn Laws', *English Historical Review*, lxxxii, 1967.

For mid-Victorian politics, see:

113 McCord, N., 'Cobden and Bright in Politics 1846–57' in R. Robson, ed., *Ideas and Institutions of Victorian Britain*, Bell 1967.

114 Burn, W. L., *The Age of Equipoise*, Allen & Unwin 1964, is a scholarly and subtle analysis of the balance of interests in mid-Victorian society.

115 Southgate, D., *The Passing of the Whigs 1832–1886*, Macmillan 1962.

116 Conacher, J. B., 'Party politics in the age of Palmerston', in

P. Appleman, ed., *1859: Entering an Age of Crisis*, Indiana U.P. 1959.

The concept of the 'respectable' labour aristocracy is put forward by:

117 Hobsbawm, E. J., 'The Labour Aristocracy', reprinted in his *Labouring Men*, Weidenfeld & Nicholson 1964.

118 Harrison, R., *Before the Socialists*, Routledge 1965, pp. 22–33.

Additional evidence is provided by:

119 Harrison, J. F. C., 'The Victorian Gospel of Success', *Victorian Studies*, i, 1957–8.

120 Pollard, S., *A History of Labour in Sheffield*, Liverpool U.P 1959, chapter 4

121 Barker, T. C., and Harris, J. R., *A Merseyside Town in the Industrial Revolution: St Helens 1750–1900*, Liverpool U.P. 1954, part iv.

122 Pelling, H., *Popular Politics and Society in Late Victorian Britain*, Macmillan 1968, questions the validity of the concept of the labour aristocracy.

Italy and America as democratic 'causes' are discussed by:

123 Beales, D., *England and Italy 1859–60*, Nelson 1961.

124 Adams, E. D., *Great Britain and the American Civil War*, 2 vols., Longmans 1925.

125 Pelling, H., *America and the British Left*, A. and C. Black 1956.

126 Harrison, R., 'British labour and American slavery', in his *Before the Socialists*, Routledge 1965.

127 Wright, D. G., 'Bradford and the American Civil War', *Journal of British Studies*, viii, no. 2, 1969.

For popular Liberalism and the Reform movement, see:

128 Vincent, J. R., *The Formation of the Liberal Party 1857–68*, Constable 1966. Chapter 2 is very useful.

129 Gillespie, F. E., *Labour and Politics in England 1850–67*, Durham N. Carolina 1927; reissue Cass 1967.

130 Maccoby, S., *English Radicalism 1853–1886*, Allen & Unwin 1938.

131 Saville, J., *Ernest Jones: Chartist*, Lawrence & Wishart 1952.

132 Briggs, A., *Victorian People*, Odhams Press 1954; Penguin 1965, chapter 8 for John Bright and Reform.

133 Read, D., *Cobden and Bright*, Arnold 1967.
134 Ausubel, H., *John Bright, Victorian Reformer*, J. Wiley 1966.
135 Hanham, H. J., 'Liberal organisations for working men 1860–1914', *Bulletin of the Society for the Study of Labour History*, vii, 1963.
136 Guttsman, W. L., 'The general election of 1859 in the cities of Yorkshire', *International Review of Social History*, ii, 1957.
137 Wolff, M., 'The uses of context: aspects of the 1860's', *Victorian Studies*, supplement to vol. ix, September 1965, examines the response of George Eliot, Thomas Carlyle and Matthew Arnold to the Reform crisis. See also R. Williams, *Culture and Society 1780–1950*. Penguin 1961, ch. 4, vi.
138 Herrick, F. H., 'The second reform movement in Britain 1850–65', *Journal of the History of Ideas*, ix, 1948.
139 Tholfsen, T. R., 'The transition to democracy in Victorian England', *International Review of Society History*, vi, 1961.

The attitude of parliamentary leaders is discussed by:

140 Jones, W. D., *Lord Derby and Victorian Conservatism*, Blackwell 1956.
141 Bell, H. C., 'Palmerston and parliamentary representation', *Journal of Modern History*, iv, 1932.
142 Williams, W. E., *The Rise of Gladstone to the Leadership of the Liberal Party*, Cambridge U.P. 1934.

For the Reform crisis of 1866–7, see:

143 Winter, J., 'The Cave of Adullam and parliamentary reform', *English Historical Review*, lxxxi, 1966.
144 Smith, F. B., *The Making of the Second Reform Bill*, Cambridge U.P./Melbourne U.P. 1966, is the best book on the 1867 Reform Act.
145 Cowling, M., *1867: Disraeli, Gladstone and Revolution*, Cambridge U.P. 1967.
146 Harrison, R., *Before the Socialists*, Routledge 1965, chapter 3.
147 Blake, R., *Disraeli*, Eyre & Spottiswoode 1966, chapter 21.
148 Park, J. H., *The English Reform Bill of 1867*, Columbia U.P. 1920.
149 Briggs, A., *Victorian People*, chapter 10.
150 Himmelfarb, G., 'The politics of democracy: the English Reform Act of 1867', *Journal of British Studies*, vi, no. 1, 1966.

151   Lewis, C. J., 'Theory and expediency in the policy of Disraeli', *Victorian Studies*, iv, no. 3, 1961.
152   Herrick, F. H., 'The Reform Bill of 1867 and the British party system', *Pacific Historical Review*, iii, 1934.
153   Magnus, P., *Gladstone*, Murray 1954, chapter 8.

Post-1867 politics are examined in:
154   Harrison, R., *Before the Socialists*, Routledge 1965, chapter 4.
155   Hanham, H. J., *Elections and Party Management*, Longmans 1959.
156   Feuchtwanger, E. J., *Disraeli, Democracy and the Tory Party*, Clarendon Press 1968.
157   Smith, P., *Disraelian Conservatism and Social Reform*, Routledge 1967.
158   Shannon, R. T., *Gladstone and the Bulgarian Agitation*, Nelson 1963.
159   Jones, I. G., 'The election of 1868 in Merthyr Tydfil', *Journal of Modern History*, xxxiii, no. 3, 1961.
160   Vincent, J. R., 'The effect of the second Reform Act in Lancashire', *Historical Journal*, xi, no. 1, 1968.
161   Feuchtwanger, E. J., 'The Conservative Party under the impact of the second Reform Act', *Victorian Studies*, ii, no. 4, 1959.
162   Cornford, J., 'The transformation of Conservatism in the late nineteenth century', *Victorian Studies*, vii, no. 1, 1963.
163   Feuchtwanger, E. J., 'J. E. Gorst and the central organisation of the Conservative Party 1870–1882', *Bulletin of the Institute of Historical Research*, xxxii, 1959.
164   Chilston, Viscount, *W. H. Smith*, Routledge 1965, is a biography of an outstanding middle-class Conservative.
165   Dyos, H. J., *Victorian Suburb*, Leicester U.P. 1961, examines Camberwell as a case study of the growth of suburbia.
166   Herrick, F. H., 'The origins of the National Liberal Federation', *Journal of Modern History*, xvii, 1945.
167   Tholfsen, T. R., 'The origins of the Birmingham caucus', *Historical Journal*, ii, no. 2, 1959.
168   McGill, B., 'Francis Schnadhorst and Liberal Party organisation', *Journal of Modern History*, xxxiv, no. 1, 1962.
169   Briggs, A., *History of Birmingham*, vol. ii, Oxford U.P. 1952.
170   Kelley, R., 'Midlothian: a study in ideas and politics', *Victorian Studies*, iv, 1961–2.

171 Lloyd, T., *The General Election of 1880*, Oxford U.P. 1968.

172 O'Leary, C., *The Elimination of Corrupt Practices in British Elections 1868–1911*, Clarendon Press 1962.

173 Thompson, F. M. L., 'Land and politics in England in the nineteenth century', *Trans. of the Royal Historical Society*, 5th ser., xv, 1965.

There is no monograph on the 1884–5 Reform Acts, but see **85** above, and:

174 Fraser, P., *Joseph Chamberlain*, Cassell 1966, chapter 2.

175 Jenkins, Roy, *Sir Charles Dilke*, Collins, revised edn, 1965, chapter 9.

176 Morley, John, *Life of W. E. Gladstone*, Macmillan 1903, vol. iii, Book viii, chapter 8.

For the post-1885 electoral system, see:

177 Pelling, H., *Social Geography of British Elections 1885–1910*, Macmillan 1967, is a massive and scholarly study of the constituencies.

178 Pelling, H., *Popular Politics and Society in Late Victorian Britain*, Macmillan 1968, is a collection of perceptive essays.

179 Pelling, H., *The Origins of the Labour Party*, 2nd edn, Clarendon Press 1965.

180 Blewett, N., 'The franchise in the United Kingdom 1885–1918', *Past and Present*, xxxii, 1965.

181 Jones, G. A., 'Further thoughts on the franchise 1885–1914', *Past and Present*, xxxiv, 1966.

182 Thompson, P., *Socialists, Liberals and Labour: the Struggle for London 1885–1914*, Routledge 1967.

183 Dunbabin, J. P. D., 'Parliamentary elections in Great Britain 1868–1900: a psephological note', *English Historical Review*, lxxi, 1966.

184 Glaser, J. F., 'English nonconformity and the decline of Liberalism', *American Historical Review*, lxiii, no. 2, 1958.

186 Cornford, J. P., 'The parliamentary foundations of the Hotel Cecil', in R. Robson, ed., *Ideas and Institutions of Victorian Britain*, Bell 1967, dissects the post-1885 parliamentary Conservative party. See also:

187 Guttsman, W. L., *The British Political Elite*, MacGibbon & Kee 1963.

For later changes, see:

188 Rover, Constance, *Women's Suffrage and Party Politics in Britain*, Routledge 1967, discusses the issue from 1866.

189 Butler, D. E., *The Electoral System in Britain since 1918*, 2nd edn, Oxford U.P. 1963.

The modern British Constitution can be studied in:

190 Harvey, J. and Bather, L., *The British Constitution*, Macmillan 1965.

191 Birch, A. H., *Representative and Responsible Government*, Allen & Unwin 1964.

For the social changes which underpinned political development, see:

192 Perkin, H. J., *The Origins of Modern English Society 1780–1880*, Routledge 1969.

ADDENDA

A revised version of Professor Himmelfarb's essay (150 above) has been reprinted as chapter 13 of her *Victorian Minds*, Weidenfeld and Nicholson, 1968. Her criticisms of F. B. Smith (144 above) are expanded in 'Commitment and Ideology: the Case of the Second Reform Act', *Journal of British Studies*, ix, no. 1, 1969. In the same number of the *Journal* is Dr Smith's reply: 'The "dependence of license upon faith"; Miss Gertrude Himmelfarb on the Second Reform Act'.

Two extremely useful recent articles are: T.J. Nossiter, 'Voting Behaviour 1832–1872', *Political Studies*, xviii, 1970; P.F. Clarke, 'Electoral Sociology of Modern Britain', *History*, 57, no. 189, 1972. A valuable, though somewhat indigestible, monograph on the 1884 Reform Act is: Andrew Jones, *The Politics of Reform 1884*, Cambridge U.P. 1972. For Disraeli, Salisbury and Conservative attitudes to Reform see: Robert Blake, *The Conservative Party: from Peel to Churchill*, Eyre and Spottiswoode 1970, chapters 4 and 5; Paul Smith, ed., *Lord Salisbury on Politics: A Selection from his Articles in the Quarterly Review 1860–1883*, Cambridge U.P. 1972, with a long and interesting introduction by the editor; Elie Kedourie, 'Tory Ideologue: Salisbury as a Conservative Intellectual', *Encounter*, no. 225, June 1972.

Index

157

Index